THE BIGGER PICTURE

The Essential Business Guide for Photographers

Jeanne Griffiths

PLANE TREE
PRESS

For Renée Forsyth and in memory of Ian

Cover and interior design: Rick Soldin www.book-comp.com
Cover photography: Quentin Bargate/www.brightnewlight.co.uk/Dreamstime.com
Back cover photographs: Joshua Hayes www.joshuahayesphotography.co.uk
Logo image: www.freevectordownload.com

Publishing Information

ISBN: 978-0-9570555-0-6
First published 2011 by Plane Tree Press
www.planetreepress.co.uk
Email: info@planetreepress.co.uk
Printed in Great Britain by Lightning Source
A catalogue record for this book is available from the British Library.

If you are a supplier or photo buyer and have suggestions of relevant products or services to be considered for inclusion in future editions or if there is any topic you would like us to cover in greater depth, please do email.

The publishers and author(s) have done their best to ensure the accuracy and currency of all the information in this book. However, they can accept no responsibility for any loss or inconvenience sustained by any reader or company as a result of its information or advice.

This book contains the names, trade marks and registered trade marks of many companies and organisations and their products, which the author and publisher acknowledge as their property. Inclusion is intended for editorial information only and in no way implies endorsement or any sponsorship by, or of, these organisations.

Contents

Acknowledgements

Many people have contributed their knowledge to this book, for which I am immensely grateful. I have used quotes and ideas from the many picture editors, photographers, stock managers and photographic tutors I have worked with or interviewed over the course of many years. Some picture editors and photographers have kindly supplied me with their words of wisdom especially for this book and I would like to thank Bryan and Cherry Alexander (Arctic Photos), Beverley Croucher, (Picture Director, *Red Magazine*); Rebecca Hawtrey, (Art Editor/Deputy Editor, *The Field*); James Mullinger, (Photographic Director, *GQ*); Polly Teller, (Picture Editor, *Sunday Times Travel Magazine*); Jayne Toyne, (Picture Editor, *Horse & Hound*) for their generosity.

I would particularly like to thank Judy Allen, Jackie Best, Renée Forsyth, Dermot Hayes and Leila Kooros who have been so supportive.

My sincere thanks also to book designer Rick Soldin, photographers Joshua Hayes, John Bulmer, Victor Englebert and all the great photographers I worked with at Time-Life. Special thanks to Robert Prior and Penny Foulkes, publishers of StockIndexOnline, who, when owners of *Hot Shoe* Magazine, set me on the road to writing about photography.

About the Author

As picture editor of Time-Life, London, Jeanne Griffiths worked with the world's top photojournalists, commissioning them for shoots all over the world and editing their work for publication. She is the author of six non-fiction books, including *The Photographer's Project Book* and editor of eight anthologies. She was a regular contributor to *Hot Shoe* magazine.

Jeanne was the editor *Country, In Business, Business Matter, Designer* and *Money Matters* magazines, commissioning both writers and photographers. She also takes photographs to accompany her articles on subjects as diverse as Lipizzaner Horses and a portrait of the Nile.

For the last fifteen years, she has been consultant editor to several major magazine publishers, launching and editing magazines on business and personal finance. She lives in London.

Preface

If you believe the many photographic forums, we may be at saturation point of the sheer number of photographers trying to earn a living. It has never been easy to make it as a photographer and it's now even more difficult. Every year, more and more photography students leave college and university. Talented amateur photographers turn professional. Citizen photographers increasingly compete with the press and paparazzi. Microstock means stock prices have fallen through the floor. Fewer publications employ staff photographers and the few such jobs that are on offer attract fierce competition. That's the bad news.

The good news is that cream does rise to the top. It takes hard work, persistence and a certain amount of luck but talented photographers can, and do, make a living. While technique with even the most advanced dslr can be learnt, that something special–interpretation, creativity, the 'photographer's eye' that makes a photograph stand head and shoulders above everyone else's–cannot. Technique can be practiced and honed but the ability to interpret and to amaze through the visual image can rarely be learnt.

Most photographers are freelance and unless fortunate enough to pick a field where they are in constant demand, and/or are particularly brilliant, have to be ever more entrepreneurial. Despite the moving image, stills photography is still used in a huge variety of ways, so whatever interests you, whatever your area of image-making, you can find a market, if your work is good enough.

It is taken as read that you are good, very good, at taking photographs. This is not a 'how to take better photos' book. There is no mention of f-stops here, no photos to distract you. Photography is probably 10% photography and

90% business. Thousands of other books concentrate on teaching the 10%. This one looks at the 90%.

Producing amazing images is all very well but photographers need more business acumen than ever. Your ability to take good photographs has become almost secondary to your ability to sell yourself. The information and advice in this book is intended to help you find and create markets for your work and help you get commissions and sales.

The boring basic stuff on UK tax, law etc., will help prevent you making fundamental mistakes in running a business. Even if it's just you and your camera, you are a business, so you need this information. There is no room for in-depth tax or VAT rules but where needed, the websites of useful and official bodies are given.

I have met many photographers who, despite their talent, have all but given up. They wait for work to fall into their laps. It no longer works like that. You need some get-up-and-go; you need to be persistent; you need to be an entrepreneur, studying and exploiting potential markets; you need to network and get referrals. No-one said it would be easy. If it were easy, anyone could do it.

Chapter One

Being In Business

As a freelance photographer, you may not consider yourself a business, but you are. It's that 90% business, 10% photography, so the more you know about the business side, the greater your control over it. You may think you can survive picking up a few commissions and selling a bit of stock, but it might not be enough to allow you to continue as a photographer. It certainly won't be the route to riches.

On many photographic forums and in interviews, even established photographers say they wish they had taken a business course or studied business books and websites early on in their careers. But it never too late (or early) to learn. Business Link is closing its regional offices and help lines but still intends to offer advice via its website, *www.businesslink.gov.uk*. HMRC's website, *www.hmrc.gov.uk*, offers advice on tax and VAT. Banks also produce free guides for new/small businesses. There are also several small business websites for the UK as well as many detailed books.

Business Plans

It is often said that a business which fails to plan, plans to fail. A business plan can help you clarify your ambitions. It can help you determine where you want to be by when and how much you need to make to afford that sports car or even to just survive. Your plan needn't be complex nor is it set in stone but it is a useful exercise.

1. You start with a summary, called an executive summary.
2. Explain what your business is.
3. Give your business entity (i.e. sole trader, partnership or limited company) and how it will operate and who is involved.
4. Include your skills (photographic, IT and business) and those of any others involved (assistants, companies to which you will outsource, such as accountants, agents, etc).
5. Briefly describe in which markets you will offer products and services
6. Outline your main competitors.
7. Write a bit about where you will operate from (it might be your home, a shared office, a studio).
8. Describe your financial and photo management systems and software.
9. Sum up your capital costs (cameras, lights, computers etc) and fixed outgoings—rent, rates, phone, broadband, insurance, travel (leave out any guess at expenses for commissioned jobs—you will hopefully be reimbursed these expenses by the client)
10. Describe how you intend to reach your market—whether marketing yourself through a website, seeing people etc., or using an agent, working through a press agency, selling stock photos.
11. Put an estimate of how much you will charge –your price list for commissions. If you intend to sell prints and/or products, add your price list and estimate sales.
12. Then comes the fun bit. Estimate how much you think you may earn, your financial forecast, in sales in years 1–5. It should include your proposed fee structure for commissioned work. You can also estimate other future sales, such as stock photography sales.
13. A one year, three year and even a five year plan is a good idea.

If you want a loan for business, to buy a studio lease/camera gear/car etc, a business plan is essential. Banks and funders will demand one. If you don't know the answer to these questions, make your best guess based on your research of markets or do more research. Making realistic estimates is one of the benefits of writing it in the first place. Review your plan after year one. You may be more or less successful than you hoped and may need to consider other fields of photography or related work, so adjust your plan.

The process of writing your plan will focus your mind on how your business needs to operate to give it the best chance of success. In the plan itself, you then go into greater detail for each section. If nothing else, it gets you researching potential markets and considering your prices.

Fortunately, help is at hand. Many banks, small business sites and Business Link offer guidance and often free downloadable templates for writing a business plan.

Get Business Savvy

You can outsource a lot of the work needed to be in business, such as bookkeeping, accounts, using an agent etc. You can ask family and friends to help out, or hire assistants, stylists etc., by the hour or by the job. It helps keep your overheads low, controls cash flow, while freeing you to do what you want to do, which is take photographs.

Some photographers are successful enough to employ assistants, secretaries and even someone to act as their agent, solely for them. However, employing people brings a lot of responsibility, not just the pressure of earning enough to pay them. You usually have to operate a PAYE system, (you can outsource to firms who will do this for you, or your accountant may be able to do it). You need to understand and comply with employment regulations, health and safety regulations, learn how to handle disputes and how to hire and fire. There is also the danger that you have to work so hard just to pay staff and rent that you never have any time for yourself or you find yourself becoming more a manager than photographer. You may increase your turnover but you may also make less profit than if you were on your own.

A little self-knowledge...

Which market or markets should I concentrate on?
What are my strengths?
What are my weaknesses?
What are the strengths of my competitors?
What are their prices?
How do they add value?
How can I add value?

Is my marketing strong enough?

Do I market myself often enough?

Would outsourcing some business aspects, to an accountant or agent, allow me to grow the business?

Can I afford to employ someone? Would a personal or photographic assistant help me expand my business?

If I expand, will I be spending less time taking photographs and more time on paperwork?

Am I charging too much or too little?

Am I exploiting this market to the full?

Is there a more lucrative field of photography?

If you do find your business growing at a fast rate, and maybe even turning away work, work smarter, not harder. You might consider raising your prices. Certainly, you will lose some clients but find and keep enough willing to pay your higher prices and you might be making the same, if not more, for less work.

It does depend on your field of photography and where you position yourself in the market. In some markets, there will be no option but to work or sell for what people will pay. In others, especially fashion, commercial and advertising, you may find pricing yourself higher will actually raise your status and your value in a client's eyes.

Everyone will expect to pay more for photography by a name than for an unknown, so getting known is vital. You want to aim to become the equivalent of a brand. Just like handbags—there's the £3000 branded version and the not-so-different high street version for £50. The expensive bag has to sell far fewer than the high street version to achieve higher profits, even though it cost more to produce.

Long Term Thinking

You may make a good living. You may make a great living now but it is only going to get harder. This author knows many great photographers, some of them pretty big names, who are living in near penury. Don't let it happen to you.

Many photographers get to a stage they think their photo collection will be worth a fortune and they can retire to that sunny beach. Sadly, with so many photographs for sale, some for peanuts and many thousands added to stock libraries every day, it is rarely the case. Maybe a stock library will snap up your work but the price for collections, unless you are a very big name (in which case you probably don't need this book), is not going to keep you in Ferraris.

If you are self employed and no employer is helping you on the pension ladder, do at least ensure you pay enough National Insurance Contributions, so there is some safety net when you retire. You could start a pension fund although the older you are, the more expensive it is—you have to contribute much more to get the same returns as if you had started one when young. However, returns on private pensions, as everyone knows, are rarely guaranteed. Very few investments are.

You could think about other options. Property may have been through a dip, but it can serve as a form of pension. If you can save enough for a deposit, buying a studio may be a wise move. By buying the freehold or long lease, you may be able to rent it, or part of it, out full time, by the day or hour. If no photographers are interested, a prop maker, an artist or other freelancer/ small business might be. Work the finances right and it may give you a studio space for free, plus an investment for which others are kindly paying.

Of course, all commercial or domestic property can be a straight buy-to-let, though it means you have the responsibilities of a landlord, even if you employ a management company. If you buy a leasehold, it may be worth exploring paying to extend the lease as the eventual sale price may more than cover this cost. There are tax and capital gains tax (CGT) implications in buying and selling, so do take professional advice from an accountant.

Whatever it is you decide to do, plan ahead. Retirement may seem a long way off but don't make planning for it your lowest priority. However, right now you also need to get work, create work and find your market.

Ten tips

1. Follow your photographic interests and find your market—don't try and be a jack-of-all trades. Specialists are invariably more successful.
2. Keep control of your money—keep accounts, chase invoices, set at least 20–25% aside for tax, or 40–50% if you are doing well (ask your accountant what your tax rate is). Put it in an instant access interest-paying account.
3. If you are VAT registered, don't spend the VAT you are paid.
4. Try to build a rainy day fund of at least three month's expenditure (to cover your rent, rates, food, bills).
5. Learn another language, improve your IT skills, especially in photo editing software—it expands your employability.
6. Network—every contact is a potential client
7. Keep your website and blog fresh and up-to-date.
8. Think outside the box—create work, rather than waiting for it to come to you.
9. Exhibit, enter competitions, comment on forums and blogs, list your services on as many website directories as you can—get known.
10. Enjoy, keep banging on doors and keep shooting.

Chapter Two

Fields of Photography

Finding Markets

Whatever your field of photography, there is a market. Within each market, you need to find the names of buyers. It may be the name of the art director, picture editor, editor, art buyer, creative director, picture researcher, picture manager, marketing manager, designer, press officer or agent. Names are found on mastheads of magazines, in directories, in trade journals, on the websites of associations and through networking. Without the name of a real person to contact, you are not going to get very far.

It would be impossible to list every art director, picture editor etc., but by using the websites listed you can find the names of appropriate organisations, giving company names. On the website of each company, you can often find the name of the right person to contact. If there is no contact name, the website will give an enquiry email address or the telephone number of a department or even the switchboard number. It is worth spending some time researching names and contact details to build your own database of contacts.

Big fish, small pond, or small fish, big pond

You can chose to specialise and most photographers do at some stage—they become known for excellent work in one field and tend to get more work in the same field as a result. Some specialise in a couple of fields that naturally go together, such as portraits and weddings or wildlife and landscapes. Some photographers even specialise within those fields.

This is not to say you can't have several areas of specialisation. Some photographers have separate portfolios and even separate websites and letterheads/cards for each field in which they work. If someone wants a portrait photographer, they will be less convinced by one whose portfolio and/or website comprises mostly sports shots.

If you are a photographer in X and Y fields, market each separately. It will get you more work. Don't call yourself a photographer and designer: in the client's eyes, you simply devalue your worth as either.

Should You Specialise?

Specialising is good. Choose a subject that you are passionate about, but make sure there is a realistic market for the images you produce. The income you will receive from your photos if you decide to specialise in photographing barn doors is unlikely to pay many of your bills!

—Bryan Alexander, Arcticphoto.com
Bryan & Cherry Alexander specialise in Cold. Whether it's icebergs or igloos, polar bears or penguins, they've shot it. Within 'cold' they shoot landscapes, towns, people and wildlife. Their work has been published in top quality newspapers, magazines and books worldwide and they run their own stock library, Arctic Photo.

Submissions–Technical Requirements

Photographers should ensure they meet the technical requirements of agencies, stock libraries and publications, which will specify submission requirements for photos in a certain dpi/size. Some, including some stock libraries, even specify which dslrs they accept.

Most computers save digital photos as RGB (red-green-blue) and publications and agencies may ask for them to be already converted to CMYK (cyan-magenta-yellow-black)—the system used by most professional printers.

There is excellent software available that will enable you to do this as well as help you manage your photographs including:

Adobe Photoshop/Adobe Lightroom
Capture NX Nikon's software
Capture One
Aperture
Microsoft Expression Media 2
HindSight
Photobyte
PhotoMechanic
ImageIngester
BreezeBrowser
Cumulus Asset Management software
Portfolio Asset Management software
DXO Optics Pro
Silkypix Developer Studio
DAM Useful Digital Asset Management and Workflow Software
ACR (Adobe Camera Raw) Digital camera raw file support

If you don't have software to convert RGB into CMYK, you can try, for free, GIMP, *www.gimp.org*, which can handle large sizes and hundreds of photos. For just a few photos, try *www.cmykconverter.com* or *www.rgb2cmyk.org*.

For technical information on the production for digital imagery, especially for print, such as dpi, sharpening, calibration, digital imagery management, RAW, TIFF and Jpegs etc., see Universal Photographic Digital Imagery Guidelines on *www.updig.org*.

The Professional Publishers' Association, *www.ppa.co.uk*, has two useful sub-sites on technical requirements for print: *www.pass4press.com* and *www.pic4press.com*.

The Professional Association of Garden Photographers also has a useful summary of guidelines of technical matters for press: *www.gpauk.org*.

www.computer-darkroom.com is another useful site for digital production.

File Transfer Protocol

Most agencies, publishers and stock libraries use File Transfer Protocol, FTP, a software system that allows you to quickly send multiple images over the internet and for the agencies, publishers and stock libraries to receive them, without the need for laboriously sending huge pictures by email.

There are lots of FTP suppliers and a few offer free services, usually with limits. Popular suppliers include Photomechanic, Fotostation Transmit, YouSendIt, Fetch, Firezilla, CuteFTP, Smartftp, Coreftp and Cyberduck (Mac users). Agencies and publications may require you to ensure your FTP system is compatible with theirs. You will need a laptop, 3G or dongle.

Importance of Captions

It is very important, especially if you are not accompanied by a writer, to have good captions, including names of people and places, with correct spelling.

If you are worried about the spelling of a name you have written down, show it to that person for confirmation that it is correct. Sometimes it is necessary to go beyond getting a name, place and date/time. You may need age, profession and where the subject(s) live. Journalists use the five Ws: who, what, where, when and why, although How is also important.

It doesn't matter too much if you are not a natural writer—most sub-editors can knock any copy into shape, so long as they have the facts.

Also see **Model Releases**: generally, press and editorial photographs do not need a model release.

Transmitting

You may have seen photographers at big football games and major events accompanied by a person operating a laptop. This is called 'teching'—when deadlines are tight, the photographer has someone there working on a laptop to deal with image processing and transmitting, which frees the photographer to keep shooting.

Press Cards

Not every photographer needs a press card and having one does not mean unlimited entry to special events. Nor will it mean you can just join the bank of press photographers outside Downing Street. These photographers are accredited by their newspapers or press agencies. A press card can, however, be useful if you want to photograph a protest march, for example. The police recognise various press cards: photographers should check the UKPCA, *www.ukpressauthority.co.uk*, which lists all 'gatekeepers' of press cards recognised by the police and other UK authorities.

To get a press card, you have to join—and pay for—membership of one of the issuing bodies. For freelance photographers, the main ones are:

> The National Union of Journalists: www.nuj.org.uk
>
> British Press Photographers' Association: www.thebppa.com
>
> Council of Photographic News Agencies and Newspaper Publishers Association: both at www.newspapersoc.org.uk
>
> National Association of Press Agencies: www.napa.org.uk.
>
> Other organisations, such as the BBC and ITV, are also listed as gatekeepers.

Most press cards last two years, after which you have to prove again that you are working as a press photographer. You can only hold one type of press card at any one time.

Press cards can be useful abroad, although photographers may find they come under scrutiny and suspicion if they declare themselves press photographers. Officials may demand they have a special visa and in certain countries, a work permit.

Photographing the Royal Family

Photographers should look first at *www.royal.gov.uk*. Under its media section, you will find details of the Royal Rota Party (a pool system), which is offered to accredited photographers only.

There is a non-rota system where you either try and book a position to photograph a Royal engagement or it is on a first-come, first-served basis. You will need a recognised press card under either system. Under the heading 'search future events'—click on the signposts on the map to see who will be where and when.

If you are assigned as a host's photographer for a Royal visit, (for instance, a college, school, care home or company hires you to record the event), there are also rules and regulations–see media information on *www.royal.gov.uk* for details on etiquette, attire, usage etc.

You could also try just being in the crowd. However, etiquette is still important: no barging in front of the public to get your shot.

Press and Paparazzi Work

Press and paparazzi photography is about being in the right place at the right time, with lightning fast reactions so you catch the shot. You need to know technical stuff inside out—like driving a car, it should be second nature. You must decide whether to stay with the pack (and there will be other photographers vying for the best position at big events), or move away from it, chancing your luck that you will capture a shot that others missed. Your picture editor will expect something, preferably something good. If it is brilliant, so much the better.

What they won't want is a call saying you missed the moment because another photographer shoved his elbow in your face. The scrum of press photographers can get quite ruthless. A photo at any price? Well, not everyone works like that but you do have to compete and that does take a certain amount of determination that doesn't suit everyone. Several photographers report being deliberately tripped up and pushed out of the way, even shooting low key events.

Speed is of the essence in delivery too. The ability to react quickly and submit to a newspaper or press agency is vital. News pictures should be sent, using a File Transfer Program (FTP), to an agency or publication preferably within minutes. The older the photograph, usually the lesser its value.

If you are planning a freelance career as a press photographer, research the most likely sources of outlets (which newspapers, which agencies) well before you cover an event. Try and establish a relationship in advance, by phoning or emailing, and understand their technical and timing requirements. Always carry contact numbers/email addresses on you.

If you haven't already made contact and capture something you think is newsworthy, ring the newspaper, magazine or press agency and explain what you have shot. They will then want to see it. If they are interested, you can then negotiate the rights you are selling (or they demand), the price or percentage. If a newspaper, ask whether they will syndicate for you and what percentage you will receive of any sale. There may not be time for a signed contract, but ask for an agreement to be emailed to you. Cover yourself by emailing them that these photos are sent for sale, under the same conditions as the terms and conditions on their site or which were agreed on the phone.

Many press photographers belong to The British Press Photographers' Association, *www.thebppa.com*. If starting out, it is worth a regular look at this site, even if you don't join, as it is here that you are likely to see announcements of any trainee schemes for press photographers. You could also consider joining the National Union of Journalists, which represents both journalists and photographers, *www.nuj.org.uk*. The National Training Council of Journalists, www.nctj.com, runs accredited courses for press photographers.

Press Agencies

Press agencies are a big source of work for photographers—they may use freelancers or employ staff photographers. Some agencies specialise, for example, in sports photography or photographs of celebrities.

Try and establish a relationship with an agency, so you are not calling cold when you have an amazing newsworthy shot to sell. Some ask you to submit some work before they will consider other photos from you, although again, that unique, amazing shot will most likely be accepted.

If you capture something newsworthy, be aware that many press agencies and newspapers may have their own photographers who have taken a similar shot. However, if you are pretty certain that no-one else has that picture or it is one that can be used as a timely 'filler' (hippos fighting and a squirrel arguing with a magpie are just two that have been published in recent months), then using a press agency can be the fastest way to sell your work. Many stock libraries will also submit timely photos to the press.

For news photos, even waiting a day for a reply from a newspaper picture editor can render your picture worthless—it becomes yesterday's news. On the whole, tabloid newspapers pay more than the quality press but all sales depend on the subject of the photo.

A press agency is geared to acting fast, has all the right contacts and can contact more than one newspaper, syndicating a newsworthy picture around the world. They may sell an exclusive to one outlet or it might be sold to several. It is in the agency's interest to get the most value out of your work, as they take a cut of the selling price. How much varies, some go 50-50, some offer photographers 65-70%, others just 30-40%.

The choice of agency depends on how fast they can act, how widely they distribute and to whom. 35% may sound low but if the agency can sell your image worldwide, it can be worthwhile taking a smaller percentage. A local or 'citizen' agency may offer more initially but can they sell worldwide? Can they syndicate your photo quickly and negotiate better rates than you could achieve?

The National Association for Press Agencies, *www.napa.org.uk*, has a list of agency members, many of them regional. Some are run by photographers or fully staffed by their own photographers or have a complete roster of freelancers, and so may not be interested in contributions or handling your work. However, most are interested in a good newsworthy photograph. Some agencies are specialist, concentrating on celebrities and royalty: others specialise in sports or are general interest, so do you research on which are the most suitable.

The big wire news agencies like The Press Association (Empics.com is a PA company), Association Press, Agence France Presse, Reuters and Bloomberg mainly use their own pool of photographers, many of whom are freelancers. They may be open to approaches for photographers in locations where they have little or no coverage. It is possible to submit photos to Reuters, with its 'Your View' page, and Reuters will pay you if it is selected for use on its professional wire service. However, read the terms and conditions, and check whether you have to agree to hand over all licensing rights.

Most agencies are interested in the citizen journalist/photographer and invite people to 'sell your story' or picture. If they think they can sell it, they are interested.

The world's third largest press agencies Agence France-Presse, *www.afp.com* (with over 1400 staff and 700 freelancers) is a share holder in The Citizenside Agency, *www.citizenside.com*, which encourages professional and amateur photographers to submit work, which they then syndicate for you. Formerly called Scooplive, it pays 65% of the sales price to the photographer.

The main UK press agencies are:

Action Images: (also acts as sports arm of Reuters News Agency)
Tel: 0845 155 6352
Email: livedesk@actionimages.com
www.actionimages.com

Big Pictures (mainly celebrity/paparazzi)
Tel; 0207 250 3555
Email: sales@bigpictures.co.uk
www.bigpictures.co.uk and www.mrpaparazzi.com, especially for paparazzi shots

Camera Press
Tel: 0207 7378 1300
Email: j.wald@camerapress.com
www.camerapress.com

Capital Pictures (mainly celebrities, show business, royalty)
Tel: 0207 286 2212
Email: sales@capitalpictures.com
www.capitalpictures.com

Corbis
Tel: 0207 644 7644
Email: info@corbis.com
www.corbis.com

Epic Scotland
Tel: 0141 945 0000
Email: info@epicscotland.com
www.epicscotland.com

European Press Agency (EPA, Germany)
Tel + 49 69 244 321 800
Email: picturedesk@epa.eu
www.epa.eu

Express Syndication
0870 211 7884
Email: mark.swift@express.co.uk
www.expresspictures.com

Eyevine
Tel: 0208 709 8709
Email: info@eyevine.com
www.eyevine.com

Famous
Celebrity/royalty etc
0207 731 9333
Email: info@famous.uk.com
www.famous.uk.com

Ferrari Press Agency Ltd
Tel: 0132 262 8444
Email: news@ferraripress.com
www.ferraripress.com

Getty Images (probably the largest stock library that also sells news-worthy and sport pictures)
Tel: 0800 376 7981
Email: editor@gettyartists.com
www.gettyimages.com
for news and sport, email: editorialsubmissions@gettyimages.com
see http://editorial.gettyimages.com

Impact Photos (also Spectrum Colour Library and Heritage Pictures)
Tel: 0207 251 7100
Email: library@impactphotos.com
www.impactphotos.com

Link Picture Library
Documentary coverage worldwide.
Tel: 0208 944 6933
Email: library@linkpicturelibrary.com
www.linkpicturelibrary.com

Newscast Ltd
Portraits, corporate
Tel: 0203 137 9137
Email: photo@newscast.co.uk
www.newscast.co.uk

Nunn Syndication
Royal Family and celebrities
Tel: 0207 357 9000
production@nunn-syndication.com
www.nunn-syndication.com

Panos Pictures
Documentary
Tel: 0207 253 1424
Email: pics@panos.co.uk
www.panos.co.uk

Photoshot and World Pictures
www.worldpictures.com,
which mainly wants travel pictures.
Tel: 0207 421 6000
Email: info@photoshot.com
www.photoshot.com

Press Association images
Tel: 0115 844 7447
Email: images@pressassociation.com
www.pressassociation.com/images

Rex Features
Tel: 0207 278 7294
Email: photogs@rexfearures.com
www.rexfeatures.com

Small World News Service
Tel: 0117 906 6550
Email: pix@swns
www.swns.com

World Picture Network (USA-based)
International news and photojournalism.
Telephone +1 212 871 1215
Email: info@worldpicturenews.com
www.worldpicturenews.com

Regional Press Agencies

Bournemouth News and Picture Services
Tel: 01202 558833
Email: news@bnps.co.uk
http://bnps.co.uk

Caters News Agency, Birmingham
Tel: 0121 616 1100
news@catersnews.com
www.catersnews.com

Cavendish Press, Manchester
Tel: 0161 237 1066
Email: newsdesk@cavendishpress.co.uk
www.cavendish-press.co.uk

Central European News Ltd, Vienna
Tel: 0043 1812 1287 19
Email: newsdesk@cen.at
www.cen.at

Hard Edge Media, Scotland–Centre Press, Capital Press Agency and
Northscot Press Agency
Tel: 0141 774 6969
centrenews@hemedia.co.uk
northscotnews@hemedia.co.uk
www.hemedia.co.uk

Dennis Rice Media
Tel: 01494 863265
Email: dennisricemedia@yahoo.co.uk
www.moneyforyourstory.com

First Features Ltd
Tel: 0207 703 8000
Email: katy@weitz.net
Website: www.firstfeatures.co.uk

Flag Media
Tel: 0143 667 2874
Email: news@flagmedia.co.uk
Website: www.flagmedia.co.uk |

London Features International
Image House, Station Road, London, Greater London, N17 9LR.
Tel: 0207 723 4204
Email: james.claydon@lfi.co.uk
Website: www.lfi.co.uk

London Media Press,
Mainly press and paparazzi, photo stories.
Tel: 0207 613 2548
Email: pictures@london-media.co.uk
www.london-media.co.uk

London News Pictures
Email: press@londonnewspictures.co.uk
http://londonnewspictures.visualsociety.com
Mercury Press Agency Ltd
Tel: 0151 708 3591
Email: chrisjohnson@mercurypress.co.uk
Website: www.mercurypress.co.uk

National News Press Agency
Telephone: 0207 684 3000
Email: news@nationalnews.co.uk
Website: www.nationalpictures.co.uk.

North News and Pictures
Tel: 0191 233 0223
Email: news@northnews.co.uk
Website: www.northnews.co.uk

Press Team Scotland Ltd
Telephone: 0123 644 0077
Email: newspressteam.co.uk
Website: www.pressteam.co.uk

Ross Parry Picture Agency
Telephone: 0113 236 1842
Email: picturedesk@rossparry.co.uk
Website: www.rossparry.co.uk

Splash News & Picture Agency (USA)
Telephone: +1310 8212666
Email: urgent@splashnews.com
Website: www.splashnews.com

Paparazzi

Paparazzi work long and anti-social hours but get the right shot and it can be hugely lucrative. At night clubs and restaurants, theatres, film studios, near the front door, up a tree—you name it, the paparazzi will be there if a famous subject is. They use fast cameras and powerful flashguns, in the hope of capturing a celebrity. They invariably ride motorbikes for rapid response. Some even have their own motorbike drivers.

Paparazzi rarely attend red carpet events, as the world's official press is there. Instead, they go for the shots that aren't official. Shots that no-one else has got pay the best. They ask (and often pay) doormen, taxi drivers and 'insiders' (friends, employees) to be tipped off about where certain celebrities will be and when. Doormen, for example, expect 10% of the price that the photo sells for, and photos can sell for £100 or £100,000.

Paparazzi keep up to date with who is in most demand—they read *Hello* and *OK!* and other celebrity magazines to see who is the most newsworthy. A whiff of scandal adds to the value of a photograph of any celebrity. The picture's value also increases if the celebrity is photographed falling over, dressed as a nun...

Paparazzi must remember the laws of confidence, defamation and trespass. There is also The Protection From Harassment Act 1997. However, if you photograph a celebrity in a public place, these photographs can usually be sold to the press, so long as no injunction is in place. Newspapers, magazines and agencies are (or should be) well aware of what they can—and can't— publish and whether there are currently any injunctions or other potential problems in publishing the photograph.

While there have been high profile legal cases brought by celebrities against publications and agencies, more recently they have also been filed against the photographer. Laws differ in different countries, so a shot that cannot be used in the UK may be able to be sold to a newspaper/magazine abroad and visa versa. Be very careful photographing children of celebrities—children have extended rights to privacy.

There is also the issue of defamation—manipulate an image of the head of a celebrity onto the body of a fat person, use a look-a-like in a compromising photo, name the wrong person in a photo caption, implying they are drunk, on drugs etc. and you, the publication and/or agency could be on the way to the law courts. If the image and/or caption is perceived to have damaged the reputation of the person or persons in the photos, it could prove very costly indeed.

There are hundreds of agencies which specialise in handling paparazzi work. It has certainly got a lot tougher and more competitive to get the shots these days but there is increased demand with more magazines or sections of magazines devoted to the celebrity culture.

Splash News, Xposure, Mr Paparazzi, The Big Picture, WENN, X17, TMZ, Rex Features, Matrix Photos, Retna, Wired Image (owned by Getty), Famous, Pix.Snapper, Shooting Stars and ACE are just of few of the main agencies. Many of the agencies listed as press agencies also deal with celebrity pictures.

A lot of press and paparazzi agencies now also want video. Video sites like *www.videoforums.co.uk* occasionally carry ads for pap video photographers.

Newspapers

While there is not enough space to give the right contact for the thousands of newspapers and magazines published in the UK and abroad, it is worth including the contacts for national newspapers. Where possible, the telephone number listed here is that of the picture desk. It would be sensible to phone the newspaper to check you have the right name for the picture editor. People do move jobs.

Almost all UK bookshelf newspapers and magazines are listed on *www. mediauk.com*, which you can consult for free, although, again, you might have to ring a publication's main switchboard to find out the name of the picture editor/art director. *www.holdthefrontpage.co.uk* also publishes a list online of national and regional newspapers. The website of Editorial Photographers UK and Ireland, *www.epuk.org*, also gives the email and modem numbers for the picture desks of many newspapers and magazines.

There are also the impressive *Willings Press Guide*, *Brad* (*www.bradinsight. com*) directories and *Benns Media Guide*, which all list contacts here and abroad. They are all very expensive but a good reference library may have access. *Benns Media Guide*, for example, costs over £200 at *www.wlrstore. com*, for a comprehensive list of contacts. It also publishes other guides with named contacts for film and TV, charities etc.

Other companies selling media databases, which also cover industries such as advertising, include *www.vocus.com, www.mediacontactspro.com and www.bikinilists.com*. In the USA, there are directories such as the Guilfoyle Report (*www.agpix.com*).

There is an association of picture editors, The Picture Editors Guild, although its website, *www.piced.net,* doesn't give much clue as to who its members are.

Rates paid for newspaper photographs vary greatly. Obviously, a scoop in the right paper can be worth thousands while a shot of someone who has turned 100 which you sell to your local paper will be worth much less. (See **Rates of Pay**).

Nationals

Daily Express
Tel: 020 8612 7000
Picture Editor: Neil McCarthy
Email: expresspix@express.co.uk

Daily Mail
Tel: 020 7938 6000
Picture Editor: Paul Silva
Email: pictures@dailymail.co.uk

Daily Mirror
Tel: 020 7293 3000
Picture Editor: Ian Down
Email: picturedesk@mirror.co.uk

Daily Sport
Tel: 0161 236 4466
Picture Editor: Paul Currie
Email: pictures@sportnewspapers.co.uk

Daily Star
Tel: 020 8612 7382
Picture Editor: Rob Greener
Email: rob.greener@dailystar.co.uk

The Daily Telegraph
Tel: 020 7931 2000
Picture Editor: Kim Scott-Clark
Telegraph Magazine, Picture Editor: Cheryl Newman
Email: photo@telegraph.co.uk

The Financial Times
Tel: 020 7873 3151
Picture editor: Jamie Han
Email: jamie.han@ft.com

The Guardian
Tel: 020 3353 4070
Picture Editor: Roger Tooth
Email: pictures@guardian.co.uk

The Independent
Tel: 020 7005 2830
Picture Editor: Lynn Cullen
Independent Magazine Picture Editor: Nick Hall
Email: picturedesk@independent.co.uk

The Sun
Tel@ 020 7782 4199
Picture Editor: John Edwards
Email: pictures@thesun.co.uk

News International owns The Sun and The Times, as well as US titles. It closed The News of the World in July 2011. Its supplement magazine, Fabulous, is now published with the Sun, and its picture editor is Kim Mayers.

The Times
Tel: 020 7782 5877
Picture Editor: Paul Sanders

The Times Magazine Picture Editor: Graham Wood
Email: pictures@thetimes.co.uk

Scottish Daily Newspapers

Daily Record
Tel: 0141 309 3245
Picture Editor: Alasdair Baird
Email: a.baird@dailyrecord.co.uk

The Herald
Tel: 0141 302 6668
Picture Editor: Brodie Duncan
Email: pictures@theherald.co.uk

The Scotsman
Tel: 0131 620 8560
Picture Editor: Andy O'Brien
Email: tspics@scotsman.com

National Sunday Newspapers

The Independent on Sunday
Tel: 020 7005 2828
Picture Editor: Sophie Batterbury
Sunday Magazine Picture Editor: Hannah Brenchley
Email: picturedesk@independent.co.uk

The Mail on Sunday
Tel: 020 7938 7017
Picture Editor: Liz Cocks
YOU Magazine Picture Editor: Eve George
Email: pix@mailonsunday.co.uk

The Observer
Tel: 020 3353 4304
Picture editor: Greg Whitmore
The Observer Magazine Picture Editor: Matthew Glynn
Observer Food Magazine Picture Editor: Kit Burnet
Email: picture.desk@observer.co.uk

The People
Tel: 020 7293 3901
Picture Editor: Mark Moylan
Email: pictures@people.co.uk

Sunday Express
Tel: 020 8612 7172
Picture Editor: Terry Evans
Sunday Express Magazine Picture Editor: Jane Woods
Email: sundayexpresspix.co.uk

Sunday Mirror
Tel: 020 7293 3335
Picture Editor: Ivor Game
Celebs On Sunday Picture Editor: Jo Aspill
Email: pictures@sundaymirror.co.uk

Sunday Sport
Tel: 0161 236 4466
Picture Editor: Paul Currie
Email: paul.currie@sportsnewspapers.co.uk

The Sunday Telegraph
Tel: 020 7931 3542
Picture Editor: Mike Spillard
STELLA Picture editor: Anna Murphy
Email: stpics@telegraph.co.uk

The Sunday Times
Tel: 020 7782 5666
Picture Editor: Ray Wells
Sunday Times Magazine Picture Editor: Monica Allende
Email: pictures@sunday-times.co.uk

National Sundays in Scotland

Scotland on Sunday
Tel: 0131 620 8438
Picture Editor: Alan Macdonald
Email: sospics@scotsman.com

Sunday Herald
Tel: 0141 302 7876
Picture Editor: Elaine Livingstone
MAGAZINE Picture Editor: Leanne Thompson
Email: sunday.pictures@sundayherald.co.uk

Sunday Post
Tel: 01382 223131
Picture Editor: Alan Morrison
Email: mail@sundaypost.com

Editorial Photography

This is similar to photojournalism for markets—magazines, newspapers and websites all run articles that need illustrating. Sometimes a photo can spark an idea for a feature which you can suggest to an editor, or they might see your work on the web, or in your portfolio and suddenly one good photo leads to a story idea and a sale or commission.

Nothing beats browsing in quality newsagents to see the huge range of magazines available and to see what is used and how. Many photographers keep reference copies of magazines that might be relevant to their potential services or sales. The name and address and the contact name (usually the picture editor or art director) can be found on the magazines' 'mast heads', usually in the front pages. The websites of some magazines and newspapers also give submission guidelines.

There is a very good association which is free to join, Editorial Photographers UK and Ireland, *www.epuk.org*. Its website has lots of useful articles and advice on law, copyright, contracts and business.

The trade body of UK magazines is the Periodical Publishers' Association, see *www.ppa.co.uk*, where you can find a list of members and their publications. You can also find a list of over 3000 magazines in the UK under numerous categories on www.newsstand.co.uk

To see American magazines, visit *http://issuu.com*
You can view a list of newspapers and magazines worldwide on *www.w3.nexis.com*

Customer Magazines–Contract Publishing

However, bookshelf publications are only half the story of UK magazine publishing. Not all publications are on the bookshelf: many are given away for free or posted. Customer magazines are not often included in media lists yet they also use photographers. If you have ever wondered who produces those magazines for supermarkets, banks, fashion chains, retail stores, estate agents, airlines, car companies, building societies etc., chances are they are produced by customer magazine publishers, sometimes called contract publishers or media agencies.

They produce business-to-customer (B2C) or business-to-business (B2B) magazines, some of which have huge print runs. (This author once edited a glossy, colour magazine for a building society which had a print run of over five million). Some of the big publishers of magazines you see in the newsagent also have customer magazine publishing divisions. Many contract publishers also produce websites for clients.

Although budgets have tightened, hundreds, if not thousands, of commercial companies still publish these magazines, produced for them by these agencies. Customer magazines all carry subtle (or not so subtle) messages of the client's other products and are used to cross-sell and to enhance brand loyalty. They all use photographs, both stock and specially commissioned work.

Magazines are proactive whereas websites are reactive—businesses have an almighty job to get people to read their websites for pleasure and not just for the information they need. People will usually, however, read free magazines, which may well spark interest in a new product or service featured.

Such magazines can also make readers feel they have made the right choice of company—whether for their money or health insurance.

Some smaller trade B2C and B2B publications are posted to members and may pay very little for photos, whether commissioned or from a stock library. However, the bigger ones, published for companies such as Royal Bank of Scotland, British Airways, M&S, Boots, Volvo, Virgin Media, BUPA, etc, need very high quality photography and are prepared to pay for it. Certainly, they use stock images but they also commission. The art directors will organise shoots for food, portraits of the celebrities interviewed, fashion, property and cars, for which they need good photographers.

Do visit the publishers' websites first, as companies move their publications from one contract publisher to another with alarming regularity. Depending on the size of the contract publisher, there may be more than one art director/picture editor–they frequently work on several titles each, as these publications are often quarterly, not monthly.

Some publishers use freelance designers who may be responsible for commissioning photography and a call to the publisher's switchboard should give you a name for the appropriate magazine. Even if it is a freelance designer you need to contact, you can write to them (and usually email them) at the publisher's office. Most customer magazines are run in small teams, with an editor for each publication and an overall editorial director or creative director of the publishing company, who you can contact if you cannot find the name of a designer/art director. Be aware that one editor may edit several titles within the group.

There is little point in contacting a big business, like the bank or supermarket, direct—they will only redirect you to their publisher (for magazines) or advertising agency.

The main contract publishers in the UK are:

Archant Dialogue–www.archantdialogue.co.uk

August Media–www.augustmedia.com

Axon Publishing–www.axonpublish.com

BBC Customer Publishing –www.bbccustomerpublishing.com

BCB & Associates—www.bcbassoc.co.uk

Bladonmore—www.bladonmore.com

Caspian—www.caspianmedia.com

Cedar Communications—www.cedarcom.co.uk

Conde Nast Contract Publishing—www.condenastcontractpublishing.co.uk

Dennis Communications—www.denniscommunications.com

Fitzgerald Shurey Tarbuck LLP–www.fitzgeraldshurleytarbuck.co.uk

Future Plus—www.futureplus.co.uk

Grist Publishing—www.gristonline.com

Haymarket Network—www.haymarketnetwork.com

Illustrated London News Group—www.iln.co.uk

Indigodog Publishing Ltd—www.indigodogpublishing.co.uk

John Brown—www.johnbrownmedia.com

Northstar—www.northstarpublishing.com

PSP Rare—www.psprare.com

Publicis Blueprint—www.publicis.co.uk

Redactive Media Group—www.redactive.co.uk

Redhouse Lane—www.redhouselane.com

Redwood—www.redwoodgroup.net

River Publishing Ltd—www.therivergroup.co.uk

Seven—www.seven.co.uk

Specialist—www.specialistuk.com

Story Worldwide—www.storyworldwide.com

Summersault—www.summersault.co.uk

Sunday Publishing—www.sundaypublishing.com

The Church of London—www.thechurchoflondon.com

The Marketing Café—www.themarketingcafe.net

Think Publishing—www.thinkpublishing.co.uk

Wardour—www.wardour.co.uk

White Light Media—www.whitelightmedia.co.uk

The Association of Publishing Agencies lists its UK and overseas members: www.apa.co.uk

You can find a list of customer (contract) publishers for the USA on www.customcontentcouncil.com

Photojournalism

This is one of the hardest areas to break into and there seems to be diminishing demand as video and television dominate, although some magazines, such as *National Geographic, The Sunday Times, Stern, Geo* etc still buy whole photo stories, often with just captions provided by the photographer.

It is one of the few areas of photography where there should be little or no altering of the image by software. Although the photographer's eye is selective, even cropping the image may lead to a 'dishonest' picture. Your photos should, as far as possible, tell the truth.

For magazines, photographers may go on a story with a commissioned freelance or staff writer. Both photographers and writers can suggest stories or the magazine editor may have an idea, and commission both writer and photographer. It is quite difficult selling a story idea without already having the photos to show, but it is not impossible. Always present a written proposal of your story idea, with your name and date on each page. It is almost impossible to prove a verbal proposal for a story idea was yours.

Some photographic representative agents may also help you sell a story but, of course, it invariably means funding the cost of the shoot, travel etc., yourself, with the gamble of finding a buyer. Selling an idea and getting a commission is safer. You can also approach a press photo agency and take advice about the potential of your story to find markets.

You stand a better chance of being published if you can take photographs that tell a story concisely, maybe offering a picture editor 20-30 selected pictures as a sequence, from which they select maybe six—or even just one and a caption. Each image should add to the story, to the other pictures and text and not just repeat information.

If you can write, you may be able to sell a whole package of words and pictures, and although rare, it is possible. Study potential markets before you write and to see their approximate word count for stories. For newspapers, 500-600 words is common. Most magazines run to no more than 1000 words, though a few in-depth features may run to 2-3000 words. A good sub-editor can always cut your text, though it is much harder for them to lengthen a story if the words aren't there.

You might consider joining The British Press Photographers Association, *www.thebppa.com*, The National Union of Journalists, *www.nuj.org.uk* if you feel a press card would be useful. There is also Editorial Photographers UK, *www.epuk.org*. All give advice on law, copyright etc., on their websites.

If you are starting out and want to study photojournalism, there are specific photojournalism courses available. Degree course are listed on *www.ucas. com* and there are some industry-based and private training courses (see **Students**).

See **Editorial** for how to find outlets.

Working 'on spec'

If you are working 'on spec' that is, doing a shoot without being commissioned, you need to get your photographic story in front of the picture editor, art director or editor. For smaller trade magazines it will usually be the editor if there is no art director. Most will want exclusive first use rights or if in the UK, at least first time UK rights.

Look at magazines that might be interested and find out the name of the right person (or phone the switchboard).

Make contact with the editor/picture editor/art director by telephone or email. If you email, put one or two reduced size photographs in the body of the email. Keep the email short and to the point (they do not want to know that you were having a great holiday when your car broke down and you came across this amazing man who told you that...).

If a magazine does take your photographic story, it may want the rights to syndicate it as well, which means the publishers will take a cut (often a large cut) if they sell it (usually to foreign publications), so check their terms and the rights they want to buy. Insist on a byline (your name credited to the photos). It's a bone of contention that photographers often get very small bylines whereas writers' names feature large in the standfirst (the paragraph below the story heading). There is not a lot you can do about this, although it is heartening to see some magazines, such as *The Sunday Times Magazine*, featuring the name of the photographer alongside that of the writer,

How to find stories to shoot

Your photographic essay should cast new light on a subject and tell a story, preferably one that has not been recently published. The photos need to be informative, stir emotions, be visually arresting and of course, technically perfect.

A simple assignment could be to find an old postcard of a place, and revisit it and photograph it today—an ideal story for the local newspaper. Major anniversaries of the birth or death of famous people and events can also trigger photo essays.

Magazines have run photographic essays and books have been published on, for example, traditional craftsmen at work, the construction of a building, the demise of an area/industry, the sunrise motive found around Britain, seaside piers and the St George Flag on everything from teacups to tattoos. The wide variety of picture essays published proves it doesn't have to be a photo essay on a hidden tribe in Papua New Guinea. Stories are on your doorstep.

Look back through some of the great Magnum photographers' stories and often (war zones apart) they cover the quite mundane. A decline of a coal mining town, the life of a crofter, the gentrification of an area, portraits of the elderly in a care home. What is important is that each picture tells its own story and together with the other photos, they make more than the sum of their parts.

Deadlines

Timing still matters although with some photojournalistic stories, it is less important than press work. It depends if it is newsworthy or whether it is something seasonal like an annual rounding up of reindeer.

Remember the lead times for magazines—most big monthly magazines start planning their Christmas issues in summer. Big magazines also tend to publish half way through the previous month, so the July issue is published in the second half of June.

Smaller magazines tend to run to the wire, publishing at the last minute to get as much advertising in as they can but if monthly, they too will have deadlines at least a couple of weeks before publication. If the magazine or newspaper is weekly, do find out their press date (often a Thursday). No-one will see you or appreciate calls on that day.

Always have a few self-portraits to hand—many magazines feature their contributors on the contents page.

Sports

Not only do newspapers have their own sports photographers, they rely heavily on freelancers selling to them directly or through press agencies. There are also agencies that specialise in sports, such as *www.colorsport.co.uk* and *www.actionimages.com*. Some agencies concentrate on one sport, such as football or racing. Others may cover all or some sports in one geographic area. These are invariably started by photographers, sometimes taking on new staff but many also use freelancers.

Quite apart from the hundreds of sports photos published every day in newspapers, there are magazines covering every sports, from the monthly *Air Gunner*, to the monthly *Wisden's Cricketer*. Whether covering athletics, golf, badminton, rugby, field sports, tennis, football, golf, darts or motorsport, whatever the sport, there is invariably a magazine. There is even a magazine for pigeon racing. A few magazines are now published solely on line. There are also the fanzines, mostly published by football clubs or produced on their behalf by customer magazine publishers.

You will need accreditation from an agency or newspaper to get in the front row among all those super-long lenses at big events. Freelancers without accreditation are very rarely considered. However, while all the main wire/press agencies will have photographers on, say, Centre Court at Wimbledon, they may just want someone to cover a junior event elsewhere. It's worth asking. Your portfolio/website will need to convince them that you have what it takes: the ability to capture action that is sharp and to transmit your work fast.

Many big sports clubs have their own 'official' photographers, often freelancers but occasionally on staff, taking photos which are used for distribution to newspapers, for PR and marketing, selling to fans and increasingly, for images on products, and their own archives. Clubs will also want photos of trainers, managers, chairmen etc., as well as formal shots of the players, for their own boardrooms and annual reports.

Most photographers cut their teeth at smaller events, to build their portfolios. Local papers often rely on freelancers (budgets are so tight that staff photographers on local papers are increasingly rare), so there may be a market there. The sportsmen or clubs may also buy your work.

Not all sports photography will be action shots: portraits of sportsmen or women at home to go with an interview or a shot of them in training can also find markets.

If there is a rising star you have spotted or heard about, you might contact them directly and request a photo shoot (the request may well be passed onto their parents or coach, if they have one). Even if you cannot find a market for it today, if that young person becomes successful, an early set of photos will have a value. You will need a signed model release (see Model Releases).

You should also keep an eye on *www.sportsjournalists.co.uk*. It recently carried an ad looking for a trainee sports photographer with the Daily Mail. Another site, *www.photographers.co.uk*, recently carried a job ad for a sports photographer in the Glasgow area.

The National Council for the Training of Journalists runs courses in press photography and photojournalism, *www.nctj.com*.

It can be worth joining a professional association, for advice, networking/contacts and press cards. The main one are:

The National Union of Journalists, *www.nuj.org.uk*

The British Press Photographers' Association, *www.thebbpa.com*

There is also The Society of International Sport & Leisure Photographers. *http://sislp/com.*

Events

Every year in the UK, there are thousands of conferences, gala dinners, charity events, awards ceremonies in every conceivable industry—all of which require a photographer's services. While some businesses and charities will organise the events themselves, bigger organisations tend to use specialist event agencies or their public relations agency—and it is these agencies that you want to target.

You could also try the marketing manager at your local large hotels and conference centres—they invariably want a few photographers' names to offer to organisers who may be new to the area. Leave a few cards with each.

Some organisations holding an event will also ask for it to be filmed but usually in addition to a photographic record.

The Association of Event Organisers: www.aeo.org.uk has a list of member companies.

The White Book is the bible for event organisers, www.whitebook.co.uk

The Events Industry Alliance: www.eventsindustryalliance.com,

The Event Suppliers and Services Association: www.essa.uk.com

The Association of Event Venues, www.aev.org.uk and www.hospitalitynet.org list the main venues

Event magazine: www.eventmagazine.co.uk

Event photographers also have their own association: The Society of International School & Event Photographers, http://sisep.net.

It could also worth listing on the Event Photographer Society, www.eventphotographersociety.co.uk

Smaller Events

There is also a market for photographers for smaller events—21st birthday parties, anniversaries, Christenings etc.,—ads asking for photographers often appear on *www.photoassist.co.uk, www.gumtree.com, www.craigslist. com* etc. You can also consider advertising if it is free but it is probably not worth paying to do so.

Food Photograhy

A highly specialised area, food photographers have many tricks to make food look very appetising, from fake ice cubes (or they'd melt under the lights), to little half spheres to make bubbles in soup (if it were really bubbling, it would steam up the camera lens). They usually have their own studios. A big food manufacturer, book publisher or magazine may have its own dedicated studio, just for food photography.

The best way into this field is a, to set up your own shoots and practice food photography for stunning shots for your portfolio, and then become an assistant to an established food photographer to learn the many tricks of the trade.

There are dedicated food stylists who work, often freelance, for these photographers: it's always worth trying to make contact with them too, as they may just refer you. They are usually credited in cookery books and food magazines and you can try Google or LinkedIn.

There is a huge market for food photography from manufacturers, producers, packaging, advertising, books, magazines, and stills for TV. Consistency of style is often an important factor, so using just one photographer for a whole cookery book or a range of food packaging is not uncommon.

Sometimes a chef may require a photographer, for publicity or décor. While he or she may already have a preferred photographers, it could be worth getting to know lesser known chefs. If they land a TV series or book contract, they may insist, as they already know you, that you to take the photographs. Riding on the coat tails of others is one way to get work.

Book Publishing

This is not so much about publishing your own book (that's covered under **Publishing**) but rather photographs used in other writer's books, be they on food, travel, fashion, architecture, health, lifestyle, landscape, wildlife…there are millions of illustrated books published on every subject every year, in every country.

Most UK publishers are members of The Publisher's Association and are listed *www.publishersglobal.com*. The main UK publishers are also listed in the *Writers and Artists Yearbook* and other media directories. All publishers have websites, so you can see if they produce illustrated books using photography.

Many also attend the annual London Book Fair (in Spring) although the main trade event is the Frankfurt Book Fair, held each autumn, which publishers from all over the world attend. For photographers, there is little advantage to be gained from attending, as most publishers are very busy, selling foreign rights to books, and the people at book fairs tend not to be the ones commissioning or buying photography. The websites of the Fairs list exhibitors.

However, budgets are often very tight these days and picture researchers, who may be in-house or freelance, may be forced to use stock libraries. However, some books need consistency of style: a cookery book, as mentioned, a guide to an historic house, a sponsored book on a big company.

Some photographers team up with a writer to produce a book. A writer and photographer team can work well, as they will have discussed an approach to both text and photos. The subjects can vary hugely, from poetry books (photographer Peter Keen worked with poet Ted Hughes on one), to wildlife, travel, fashion and specific subjects such as gold or diamonds. It could be worth cultivating relationships with writers of non-fiction subjects.

There are also book packagers, firms that produce books, often to camera ready art (the book designed, the text edited and set, the photographs in place). They then sell the package to a larger publisher which prints and distributes the book. The commissioning of text and photography is usually done by the book packaging company. See the London Book Fair website for a list of the main ones, *www.londonbookfair.co.uk*.

Charities and Non-Government Organisations (NGOs)

Although many charities will want volunteer photographers, others will pay, as they need excellent photographs for fundraising material. Many photographers offer a discount to charities; others donate their time for free. It is a moot point whether you should work for free. The charity's staff are paid, so why not you? Directors and top management of charities are often very well paid and, like it or not, the charity sector is very big business.

You could offer to cut your usual day rate substantially, as long as the job is still financially worthwhile. For charity events, some photographers do not charge and instead try and sell pictures at the event. They may print out photos there and then or take orders for prints and framing for delivery later. Some charity event photographers will offer to give the charity a percentage of the sale price. For instance, one company of charity event photographers makes no charge to any charity for photographing its events but sells the photos, printed on site, for £15 each, of which £2.50 is donated to the charity.

Some charities advertise for people to go on an amazing trip abroad, where you have to pledge to raise a certain amount of money on its behalf. It can be a good way to get to travel off the beaten path, expand your portfolio and make contacts. Photographers should clarify who owns the rights to the photos as the charity may well want to use them for free. Can you then sell them as a story or put them in a stock library?

Many charities run photographic projects in disadvantaged communities across the world. Photo Voice, *www.photovoice.org*, for example, may need tutors or be open to a suggestion of a project.

Other charities, such as Save The Children and St Martins-in-the-Field run occasional photographic workshops, where you could get involved (though it is doubtful you'd be paid). Changing Ideas (*www.changingideas.org*) is open to applications for socially beneficial photographic projects and offers a residency to complete a project. You can find volunteer opportunities and list your expertise on *www.do-it.org.uk*. Organisations like VSO are also worth looking at.

You can find a full list of charities at the Charities Commission websites, www.charities-commission.gov.uk for England and Wales www.oscr.org.uk for Scotland

www.charitycommissionni.org.uk for Northern Ireland

Also see www.charitiesdirect.com and www.guidestar.org.uk

Photography for Schools and Colleges

There are many companies/photographers specialising in photographing school pupils. Some also produce year books, as well as taking a whole school/ class shots and shots of individual pupils, which pupils/parents then order, usually mounted and with the option of a framed print. It's big business. It is a well-trodden path and there is not much room for more photographers of 'formal' school shots but as existing photography companies expand, they do advertise from time to time on sites like *www.photographers.co.uk*. Sometimes, the ads are for jobs abroad in places like Hong Kong or Dubai.

Apart from the formal annual photo shoots, a school may well be interested in someone to photograph a visit by the mayor, a school play, a rugby match etc. Contact the marketing department or if there isn't one, the head teacher. Public schools (as opposed to State schools) are invariably more flexible and may have bigger budgets when it comes to using photographers.

You may need to pass some type of official check if working with children. A Criminal Records Bureau check or enhanced CRB is common (see www. direct.gov.uk/crb) or a check under the Vetting and Barring Scheme: *www. isa-gov.org.uk*. The photographic company or school employing you will organise this: you cannot arrange this yourself.

Entertainment

Actors, dancers, singers, musicians, comedians, circus performers and other entertainers need shots for publicity, to send to fans and sometimes, to accompany a publication/website article. Such commissioned work may mean you have to give away most, if not all, rights and may be unable to sell on the photograph for stock or to the press. There are specialist drama, music schools and courses where you can offer your services.

For performance, most photographers from newspapers and magazines are invited by the press office to attend a photo call. Usually there will be no audience, the cast will be in full make-up and costume, and theatres may raise the brightness of stage lights. It is worth contacting the theatre press and publicity department or the company manager, especially on smaller productions, to see if there is any chance you could attend a photo call and try selling the photos to newspapers and magazines.

The trade publication for the theatre industry is *The Stage*, and there are many other publications for opera, dance, music, etc, where images are used and where photographers occasionally advertise.

Photographers can also offer their services to a particular venue or a theatre/dance/music group to shoot photographs for publicity shots, posters and programmes.

Most young bands will be only too happy for you to attend a concert and take photos, as they will also need photographs (along with promotional videos) for their own marketing. If you can sell your photographs to a music magazine, they will be delighted. Some bands, having enjoyed success, will want an experienced photographer for publicity material, posters, covers etc., and it is often the manager or record label that arranges this, although they may well outsource it to a design agency.

If starting out, you might offer to take pictures at your local amateur dramatic society, dance troop, orchestra etc. You could send your card to the press officer/company manager and try and arrange to see them. You might be able to make sales of prints, perhaps mounted and framed if there is no budget to pay you a fee. Photographing amateur or semi-professional events will also give you the chance to practice. The lighting restrictions invariably mean using fast ISO speeds while trying to minimise grain. You cannot use flash during performances.

Formally photographing well-known people in the entertainment industry is difficult without a commission from a newspaper or magazine that is also running a feature on them. You can write on spec to their agents–all established actors have them, which you will find in the industry bible, *Spotlight, www. spotlight.com*, but without the article/photo commission, it is rare to get a reply.

What you can do is headshots. Every performer needs a good portrait to put in *Spotlight* and the other casting directories and websites and they need them regularly updating. Rates for headshots vary greatly—from a mere £49.00 to £290 for 200 shots. Most offer discounts of around 10% to students.

You could ask drama schools and drama departments of universities if you can put your card on their notice board. Young actors are invariably strapped for cash but know they need a good headshot, so will expect to pay. You can list your headshot service, sometimes for free, on sites such as:

> www.spotlight.com
>
> www.contactshandbook.com (the handbook of Spotlight)
>
> www.uk.castingcallpro.com
>
> www.uk.stagejobspro.com
>
> www.talentcircle.org
>
> www.starnow.co.uk (which also carries 'photographers wanted' ads)
>
> www.theactingwebsite.com
>
> www.musicwork.org
>
> www.typecaster.co.uk
>
> www.linkedin.com
>
> The following sites also carry some ads asking for photographers.
>
> www.indeed.co.uk (searches most jobs websites)
>
> www.movethat.co.uk
>
> www.gumtree.com
>
> www.creativejobscentral.co.uk
>
> Local forums and sites with the words 'music scene' and free classified ad jobs also throw up some jobs.
>
> Some entertainment sites are mainly for the USA, including www.mandy.com, www.nowcasting.com, www.actorsaccess.com, www.800castings.com www.backstage.com, www taltopia.com and www.castingcall.us

Festivals are big business: whether its modern music or classical, modern dance or ballet, art or literature, there are hundreds of festivals run every year, usually in the summer months. Festivals are also run by towns, such as the Edinburgh Festival. Of course, these are not confined to the UK. While many will be filmed, they will all need stills photography. They may have their own accredited photographers, and will almost certainly invite the press and their photographers, but some festivals are often so large they need more than one photographer. Contact the festival organisers.

Unit Stills Photographer

All film units have stills unit photographers, to photograph possible locations, to record the event, to act as a continuity recorder and to use as publicity. The photographers are usually freelance, employed just for that film or TV production. There are also several location finder companies that use photographers.

A stills unit photographer on even a modest budget film will most likely be an established photographer with a good track record. They will also be very patient. A lot of time on film sets is spent sitting around and waiting, with very early calls and working late into the night.

It is very rare for a freelance photographer to be given open access to a film or TV set, as the production company will want control of the pictures the public sees. Most film stars have the right of veto written into their contracts as to which pictures can be used. Unit photographers will also have to assign copyright, meaning they cannot then sell the pictures elsewhere.

Most of this work is through contacts—you rarely see an advertisement for a unit stills photographer. You could try contacting the unit photographers on the credits of films you like, and asking if you can assist on his/her next film job. You can also contact production (both film and TV) companies, and send an email with a link to your website. Kemps Film and Television www.kttv.com is one main industry directories and Kays is another: wwww.kays.co.uk. Many producing houses are also listed on *www.film-tv.co.uk*, *www.4rfv.co.uk* and *www.fatcat.co.uk*, while *www.theknowledgeonline.com* sells a directory of contacts.

For the sites of main associations for those in the TV, film and documentary world, such as *www.directors.uk.com*, *www.productionbase.co.uk* and *www.*

theproductionguide.co.uk. The media and entertainment union, BETCU, *www.bectu.org.uk*, has Crewbus, the directory for freelance members. BETCU also runs an annual freelancers' fair where you can make contacts. Get yourself listed on as many production directory websites as possible. For contacts, particularly overseas, try *www.mandy.com*.

However you make contact with a producer or director, it is worth including on your card/marketing material and cv any information that could be useful to a film company, such as stating you have a Full UK Drivers License, an I-Visa for USA or a PADI Under Water Instructor Certificate.

Without a track record, the larger film companies are unlikely to consider you. Depending on the film and country, you may also need to be a member of a relevant trade union.

You will need to know how to use a sound blimp—a housing attached to your camera which reduces the sound caused by the shutter click, so as not to interfere with the sound on a film set. It is also used in theatrical photography, wildlife and surveillance work.

To get a foot in the door of the film world, you could offer your services as a unit still photographer to a film or drama school, or to any young film maker or low budget film. Although working for free is to be discouraged, this will allow you to build a credible portfolio, with a mix of stills, portraits and behind the scenes shots.

Film schools such as The National Film & Television School and Central Film School may well have young directors who will want unit photographers.

You could also search the web for jobs—they are usually posted by young film makers wanting free or cheap photographers– sites like *www.indeed. co.uk* gather jobs from websites like Gumtree. You might also try listing your services on:

    www.linkedin.com

    www.shootingpeople.org

    www.talentcircle.org

    www.uk.filmcrewpro.com

    www.britmovie.co.uk

www.ukfilmlocation.com

www.ukscreeen.com

www.uk.castingcallpro.com

www.cinematography.com

There is also www.mandy.com, which has an American bias.

Glamour

There is certainly a big market for glamour shots, from Page 3 to specialist magazines, some of which could well be classified as pornographic. Look at the top shelf of any newsagents and it is crowded with 'glamour' magazines. There is also a market for photos for lad's mags, which often carry some glamour photography. Shoots are also done for lingerie, websites, adult toy catalogues and model portfolios. Some respectable organisations may also feature glamour photography.

Shoots are usually done in a studio and you will invariably need to pay the models, Some photographers offer model portfolio shoots, for which they charge the model, and reputable model agencies need photographers for portfolio shoots.

There are hundreds of model agencies that specialise in glamour models. You could also advertise for models, although you should make your intentions clear whether nudity or explicit photography is involved. Do ensure the models are over 18. These shots can also be used for your own portfolio, which you can then show to art directors. You could also try submitting pictures to appropriate publications, if you have agreement of the model and a model release.

One newspaper picture editor of a national 'red top' (the tabloid papers that use glamour/page 3 girls) said the reason she rejected most glamour photos was that the eyes of the model were 'dead'—lively eyes are essential. She also said that the girl must look, if fully clothed, like the sort of girl you'd be happy to introduce to your mother.

Depending on the level of photography and the publication, you may need the services of a stylist and make-up artist. Many stock libraries will not take glamour shots—read their submission guidelines carefully.

Commercial

Companies need photographs to illustrate brochures, websites, annual reports and for advertising. They need photographs of their top people and to accompany press releases. They may want photographs of their staff and premises for their annual reports, staff magazine or even for their walls. They need all their products photographed. They may want their services interpreted through illustration or photographs. The company may also want photographs of a project they are working on.

It is tempting to look to the manufacturers of products which we all use in the home but you are more likely to have success in finding work if you look at specialist industries. Whether it is bridge building, quarrying, farming machinery, medical equipment, a new type of gasket…it doesn't really matter what it is, but it will need photographing at some point. If starting out, a smaller manufacturer or service company may be a better bet.

Companies may have their own PR, design and marketing departments or outsource to agencies. Most companies will outsource advertising work. It is the design, PR, marketing people you want to reach. Also see **Advertising**.

Reading appropriate trade magazines, newspapers like the Financial Times, will lead you to company names or there are directories of companies in good reference libraries. You can then research the company on the web. Usually, you will find appropriate contacts under the heading 'Press' on the site. It should give you the name of individuals handling PR and/or marketing, whether in-house or outsourced.

You need a name, not just 'dear sir or madam'. It can be worthwhile using the post, rather than email, to send your promotional card with a short note, giving a link to your website. Follow it up a week or so later with an email or phone call, asking if they received it and whether they would consider using you when they next need a photographer. If approaching a company's own marketing/pr department, a line or two demonstrating your knowledge of the company/industry will help. If you have any contacts, however tenuous, use them.

If you hear of a company's interesting project, you could contact them and ask if you could photograph it. Write to the press and marketing offices if the company has them: the Managing Director if not. Writing is often a better bet than phoning, as it gives them time to consider. You should make your intended use clear—if you want to try and sell the photos as stock or to a publication, the company in question will want control of their image. However, they may be interested in buying the prints for their archives, annual reports etc. You will also need model and property releases if you intend to use the photographs commercially. See **Model Releases**.

Photographers might consider joining:

The British Institute of Professional Photographers, www.bipp.com

The Association of Photographers, www.the-aop.org

The Master Photographers Association, www.thempa.com

The Society of International Commercial and Industrial Photographers: http://sicip.net

Advertising

Advertising agencies come in all shapes and sizes. One only tends to hear about the very large ones but there are hundreds, based all over the country (not just London, although the biggest UK agencies invariably have a London bias).

Advertising photography covers everything from shots of a new car in an exotic location, to travel, food, hotels, perfume, watches, wine, shoes, fashion—whatever the product or service it invariably needs to be advertised. Although much advertising is now filmed for TV, there is still a huge market for stills. The role of advertising photography is obviously to make the product irresistible to its target market. The style of photography and where and how ads are used will reflect the demographics of the intended audience. The smaller the brand, usually the smaller the budget.

Many smaller brands may well use stock photography, sometimes in conjunction with a shot of their own product and manipulate the images on computer to create the image they want. However, art directors (who might be called creative directors or creative partners) and art buyers of advertising agencies do commission a lot of photography.

Big brands nearly always go for big names, the tried and tested photographers, as they can't afford for the photographer to mess up. It is worth looking at the work of photographers like Nadav Kander, Nick Meak, Nick Georghiou, Chris Frazer Smith, Sue Parkhill, Guido Mocafico, Nick Knight and Ben Stockley, who are among the most successful advertising photographers in the UK.

Big campaigns are not the place to try and cut your teeth. There are plenty of small agencies around the country, handling smaller campaigns, both 'above the line' (main stream) and 'below the line' (auxiliary promotion from labels and fliers, to point of sale). Build up your portfolio before you approach the major agencies.

Most art directors are open to seeing photographers they don't know but make sure your work is fabulous, both technically and conceptually.

The websites of advertising agencies should tell you the clients they have and the styles of photography they like. That is not to say they are closed to other styles: far from it. If your portfolio shows work that is innovative and amazing, it may well appeal for a future project. You won't necessarily know what campaigns they are starting on (although reading *Campaign* magazine may tell you). If your style fits what they are after or gives them ideas, they may commission you. It is worth showing a good mix of styles, without seeming a 'jack-of-all-trades'.

If starting out, set up a few shoots of products or fashion and make sure those photos shout 'I want one of those'. For travel advertising shots, the photos should say 'I want to go there'. If the agencies, as most do, offer their services to charities, the photo must say 'this makes me want to donate to that charity'.

For a list of UK advertising agencies see: *http://brandrepublic.blueboomerang. co, www.theknowledgeonline.com,* The Creative Handbook, *www.chb.com* and the Marketing and Creative Handbook, *www.mch.co.uk*

Campaign is the trade magazine of the advertising industry and you can glean a lot of contacts from it. Its website is *www.campaignlive.co.uk*. You need to register on the site to see a list of the top ad and media agencies and top 100 creative agencies. Campaign's Photo Awards winners also give you a), an idea of standards and diversity of subjects covered and b), the photographer's name and c), the agency behind the photograph.

> The Advertising Association, www.adassoc.org.uk, is a federation of 24 trade bodies, so is good starting point.

> The Institute of Practitioners in Advertising www.ipa.co.uk, has a list of members. For a list of regional advertising agencies, try www.advertisingfinding.co.uk and www.freeindex.co.uk. You will need to call the switchboard to ask the name of the creative director.

> There is also the Advertising Producers Association, www.a-p-a.net and the International Advertising Association, www.iaauk.com, the chapter of the US based IAA.

> Also see links on their websites to other useful sites, such as www.adforum.com.

In the USA,

> The American Association of Advertising Agencies, www.aaaa.org

> The International Advertising Association, www.iaaglobal.org.

> Also try www.workbook.com, but you have to subscribe for a list of contacts and to have your work and details included.

> For a list of advertising trade bodies worldwide, see www.obs.coe.net

Jobs in advertising for art directors, art buyers and computer operators of photographic editing/manipulation software (but rarely for photographers), appear in *Campaign* and *Creative Review* and on web sites like *www.creative pool.co.uk*.

Designers

Designers use photography all the time, for brochures, fliers, books, adverts, etc. They may be freelance or in a creative agency, such as an advertising, media or design agency. Depending on the job and its budget, they may commission photography or use stock.

Many designers (graphic, events, fashion, industrial, etc.,) belong to the Chartered Society of Designers—*www.csd.org.uk*. Click on 'find a designer', chose an area to search and a list of designer members comes up. Click on a name for further information and contact details. For the Directory of Design Consultants, see www.designdirectory.co.uk.

You can also find contacts on *www.designerdirectory.co.uk* and *www.design-intellect.co.uk*. Many designers also list themselves on network sites and groups on LinkedIn and Facebook.

Forensic Photography

We have all seen CSI and how crime scenes will be photographed in great detail. However, it is usually a Scene of Crimes investigator who is holding the camera. Most forensic photographers are police, military or forensic scientists first and photographers second. The UK Government is talking about disbanding our own forensic services, which means it is likely private companies will be the sole source of forensic science services. See *www.forensic.gov.uk*. Also see *www.crime-scene-investigator.net*, *www.forensic-science-society.org.uk* and *www.lgc.co.uk*.

There are even a couple of BSc degrees in the UK for forensic photography (see *www.ucas.com*)

> See *www.bjp-online* for bursaries details for forensic photographers.
>
> The British Institute of Professional Photographers, *www.bipp.com*, even has an forensic award section in its annual competition.

Investigator Photography

Private investigators use photography and video all the time. Again, most are private investigators first and photographers second. They need to understand the law concerning privacy, trespass and entrapment. The main organisations are: The Association of British Private Investigators *www.theabi.org.uk* and the Institute of Private Investigators, *www.ipi.org.uk*.

Working for the Government & Its Agencies

Government departments, government funded bodies such as museums and galleries, government agencies and the Armed Forces all employ photographers. They usually require some formal qualifications, to at least NVQ/ SVQ level. The Professional Qualifying Examination of the British Institute of Photography is well respected, as are degrees.

The Army and Royal Navy recruit their photographers from serving personnel but the RAF (*www.raf.mod.uk*) does take photographers from civilian life, though they also do a course of basic recruit training. They then attend the defence School of Photography, where they learn reconnaissance photography, aerial, equipment and portrait photography. The Ministry of Defence only recruits qualified photographers, who are then trained in Electronic News Gathering (ENG Cameraman), Video Production Training, Photo Journalism Training for Defence Media Operations or Minilab Operation.

The police use photography in surveillance and forensic work but its photographers are invariably policemen first, photographers second.

Each government department and agency has its own website where jobs are posted. It is a question of ploughing through them. You starting point could be *www.civilservice.gov.uk*.

Architectural Photography

Architects and construction companies use very good photographers to record their work throughout the build or renovation and when finished. The building needs wonderful photographs for sales brochures and websites, usually produced by the company which commissioned the building. Some large architectural firms also produce books of their work and may do so with established publishers. There are several architecture and building magazines in the UK, and many more abroad that want quality photos to accompany articles (see **Magazines**). You will need signed property releases for commercial use of most architectural photography.

There is also a demand from estate agents—the big ones often produce hand-bound limited edition books and glossy brochures of beautiful photographs of grand houses and land for sale. These photos are also used to advertise, often in magazines like *Country Life*. Smaller estate agents also need every property photographed inside and out for their office windows, websites and handouts.

Hotels also require good photography to use on websites, in brochures and for publicity. Organisations such as the Historic Houses Association, English Heritage, the Landmark Trust, the National Trust use photographs of architecture all the time.

Most photographic work for architects, top estate agencies, the National Trust etc., tends to be commissioned work rather than stock. If a phone call to reception doesn't get you the right contact, the press office is usually a good place to start: send a short email asking for a name and email address of the person who commissions photography (and always put in a link to your website). If that doesn't get you anywhere, try asking the press office to forward it to the appropriate person.

If large enough, an architectural firm may have a publications department. In smaller firms, it can be worth contacting the lead architect, by email with your website link, maybe sending a chase up email a week or two later.

You could also search for construction engineers and property developers. They may be one-man bands or huge international companies, charities, housing associations, hotels or hotel groups and, of course, government departments outsourcing the building of roads, bridges, hospitals, schools, etc. All need very good photography.

You might also try product suppliers, the companies which architects use to supply windows, tiles, wallpaper, kitchens, bathrooms, sound systems, TVs and home cinema, hot tubs, swimming pools, outbuildings, home studios, garden furniture -there are hundreds of them. They not only need photography for their own marketing but will want shots of their products in situ. It can often pay well and there are many more product suppliers than there are architects.

You can find names of architect members at

The Royal Institute of British Architects (RIBA), at www.architecture. com.

The Architectural Association School can be useful for finding young architects, www.aaschool.ac.uk.

There are also landscape architects and designers who use photography (see gardens).

See *www.bjp-online* for details of bursaries for architectural photographers. Many awards and competitions have architectural photography sections. These are run by both photographic associations and architectural magazines.

Several architectural photographers' associations are US based but do have UK members.

The International Association of Architectural Photographers, www.architecturalphotographers.org

The Association of Independent Architectural Photographers, www.aiap.net.

Photographing Interiors

There are hundreds of magazines in the UK and abroad, plus features in style colour supplements that cover homes and interior design. All need stunning pictures. They may or may not feature the property owner and different magazines have different levels of photography, according to their budgets. Even celebrity magazines run features on homes of the rich and famous and often the celebrity is paid as well. Almost all these features are commissioned—rarely do picture editors buy a feature story on a home from a library or agency. Such is the thirst for new interiors that finding a good one is in great demand.

Occasionally, a photographer can strike an agreement with an owner to approach a magazine with a view to photographing it. In this instance, the owner may well expect some recompense, although if selling up, they may agree for the free marketing publicity an article will bring. You will need a property release as well as model releases if your photographs include people. A big magazine will, if interested, assign a writer. It is very rare for a picture buyer to commission the photographer to write as well, or to ask the photographer to find a writer. Some smaller magazines, however, may well buy a package of words and pictures.

For interior designer contacts and to list your services see The British Institute of Interior Designers, www.biid.org.uk

> Interior Designers may also be members of the Chartered Society of Designers, www.csd.org.uk

> As with architecture, there are also many suppliers of fixtures and furnishings to target.

Garden Photography

Gardens feature prominently in homes magazines, as well as in, of course, gardening magazines, newspaper colour supplements, ads and books. Garden shots are also often used for cards and calendars. If photographing on spec, a magazine may send a writer later, to interview the owner and identify plants. Photographers approaching any garden owner will need the owner's permission (not just that of a head gardener, for instance) and a property release.

Gardens and plant photos are also used by garden centres and nurseries, commercial equipment suppliers, which also need their equipment, plants and premises photographed. They may also buy work through stock libraries.

To find garden/landscape designers see *www.garden-network.co.uk* for a list of most associations. Garden photographers, like many other areas of photography, have their own association, The Professional Association of Garden Photographers: *www.gpauk.org*.

Landscape

If you specialise in landscape photography, you can sell work to magazines, newspapers, travel and tourist brochures, guide books and advertising. Calendar, greeting cards and wall art companies may also be interested. It is not just countryside shots that sell—urban landscapes are as popular.

The National Trust or Sites of Special Scientific Interest, woodland and forestry organisations may well commission landscape shots, especially if they have recently acquired a property. Commercial companies such as mining and oil companies, road builders, etc., may also want photographs to show how well they are doing restoring the site back to near its original state.

There are several major landscape photographic competitions, both in the UK and internationally, which can be worth entering but do read the small print on what rights you are agreeing to by entering (this applies to all competitions).

If you are not commissioned but have some terrific landscape shots, you might try selling a one-shot photo story to a magazine or newspaper. Otherwise, to reach a wide market, your best outlet is probably a good stock library, particularly a specialist one. You may think that your photographs will just be lost amid a huge number of pictures but a picture researcher with a specific brief of a location or style of landscape photo may well look at the work in a specialist library first.

Wildlife

The same reasoning applies to wildlife photography. Picture researchers wanting a photo of the Green-winged Teal are more likely to go to a specialist photo library than a general one, especially if they can be confident the photo they are looking at is correctly captioned, perhaps with both its common and Latin name (*Anas carolinensis*).

This is also true if you have managed to photograph something quite rare. Rare sightings and unique moments (hippos fighting, an elephant fending off a lion, a falcon nesting in the centre of town) also have press value. If you do photograph something amazing that might make a good press story, a photographic agency can probably sell it to more places more quickly and at a higher price than you may be able to achieve yourself. If approaching a specialist wildlife stock library, do ask if they are proactive and also submit work for press inclusion, as you don't want to lose a sale by your photos being filed as stock. Picture editors want the story to come to them.

There are many wildlife magazines and numerous books published around the world. Tourist Boards and travel companies also use wildlife photos. Guide books may also feature wildlife photographs and although it is unlikely you could get commissioned, having your work in a specialist library can help. There are also regular wildlife photographic competitions you can enter, some of which are very prestigious, like the International Wildlife Photographer of the Year, which culminates in a major exhibition at the Natural History Museum.

Wildlife photographs also make popular subjects for calendars and greetings cards. The Natural History Museum, for example, does great trade in prints, calendars and postcards from work in its annual IWPY exhibition.

Given the difficulty of wildlife photography, publications may well use images taken from high-definition video cameras or from the video feature on some dslrs, if high enough quality.

Landscape, nature and wildlife photographers can join the Society of International Nature & Wildlife Photographers: *http://sinwp.com*

Travel Photography

Travel shots can find markets in newspapers, magazines or travel websites and while many will rely on stock these days, there is still the chance of commissions for new hotels, hotel refurbishments, hotel groups and individual hotels, airlines, tourist boards, cruise companies or holiday parks. Guide books also want travel pictures, although many publishers use stock libraries. Some, however, may want a consistent style in the book and commission. Many companies and tourist boards will outsource brochure design work and it may be the design or advertising company which commissions/buys pictures.

You can find the names of many airlines, hotel groups, cruise companies and travel companies who attend the annual World Travel Market at *www.wtmlondon.com*. From there, you need the find the name of the marketing director or art director, if they have one, or the design/advertising agency they use (it may well be more than one).

ABTA, *www.abta.com*, sells a list of its c.5000 members for £39.50. *www.hospitalitynet.org* lists all hotels groups and hospitality associations worldwide.

You can also try the Association of Independent Tour Operators, *www.aito.com* and the British Activity Holidays Association, *www.baha.org.uk*.

There are companies offering photographic holidays and some of the existing operators may be open to proposals for a new photographic holiday, with you as a guide/tutor (see **other business and work opportunities**).

Cruise ship owners employ photographers although with the advent of cheaper digital cameras, it is now less common. Some photographers on cruise ships may act as guides/teachers. There are sometimes cruise line photographer jobs advertised on *www.bjp-online.com* or try *www.cruiseshipphotograherjobs.com*. All cruise lines need photographs for brochures, advertising and the launch of new ships. There is a difference between cruise ship owners, like P&O, which will need brochures, and charter companies, like Thomson, which will invariably use photographs supplied by the ship owner. Ship owners may also commission photographs of destinations, although more and more buy from stock libraries. The annual paperback, *A Complete Guide to Cruising*, published by Berlitz Publishing, gives the name of owners of all cruise ships.

Owners of holiday villas and cottages also need good photographs. Most will attempt to do it themselves, but some may be open to professional shoots. Apart from the top end villas and houses, budgets will be tight. You could always propose a barter—a holiday in the property in return for a set of photographs.

The Society of Travel & Tourism Photographers: *http://sittp.com*

Fashion Photography

Think of fashion and we tend to think of advertising and editorial photographs in glossy magazines. Most fashion magazine editors want to see something new, a fresh style—they will have seen hundreds of Modino/Bourdin/Knight copycats.

However, there is a huge market beyond magazines. Every item of fashion produced needs photographing for websites, catalogues, PR and shop displays. Fashion photography, for fashion houses and retail outlets, as with most product photography, overlaps with advertising. Commercial fashion photography usually pays better than editorial, although the latter often carries more prestige.

Open your Sunday newspaper and chances are that a brochure from a clothing company will fall out. Some catalogues and websites can't afford the big name photographers and don't want the photographic creativity you see in fashion magazines. What they need is inspirational and fun photography, where you can see all the clothes very clearly, modelled and photographed so the clothes look good. They may be shot on location or in a studio but the one thing they have in common is clarity. Some clients are now asking for 360 degree photography for their websites.

A lot of successful fashion photographers start as assistants to established fashion photographers but some have found work through recommendations from a stylist or model with whom they have worked. A contact, however tenuous, helps you get noticed ahead of the competition and if your work is very good, a commission may follow. One top editor spotted a photographer's blog (showing amazing pictures, of course), which resulted in commissioning him for her fashion magazine. Fashion shows tend to be covered by accredited (and invited) press.

There are also many photographers/companies offering to photograph models for their portfolios. However, there is also the world of exploitation of (usually) young girls, charging them a fortune for a shoot, even if it is obvious they are not model material. These companies should be avoided.

Young photographers and students might set up their own fashion shoot. A free ad on *www.gumtree.co.uk,* or announcement on Facebook etc., for models in return for a few portfolio prints and a CD might work, but make sure it is all above board. If teenagers come forward as models, invite their mothers to the shoot. Among the annual competitions for fashion photography is the Clothes Show Live Young Fashion Photographer of the Year.

You can keep costs low by doing a location shoot, which is just as valid as a studio shoot, or borrow/hire a studio for half a day. You might get local young/student designers, hair-stylists and make-up artists wanting to practice their trade on the shoot, again in return for copies of pictures.

Fashion photographers may belong to:

The British Institute of Professional Photographers, www.bipp.com

The Association of Photographers, www.the-aop.org

The Master Photographers' Association, www.thempa.com.

> Like many professions, fashion is truly international. While English is the language of business, being able to speak another language, especially French, Italian or Spanish, can help you get work abroad.

Portraits

Portraits are commissioned to accompany articles on that person, but there is a much wider market for portrait work than magazines and newspapers. Not all companies can afford—or want—a painted portrait of the chairman but they might consider a formal photograph for the boardroom. Companies also need portraits of staff for press releases, annual reports etc.

Individuals may also want a portrait of themselves or family, especially for landmark occasions, such as birthdays, anniversaries, graduation, bar mitzvahs etc. It may be worth doing a door-to-door mail-drop, offering a shoot for a set price, stating exactly what is included in the price. People will want a fixed fee, rather than an hourly rate and package rates seem to work best.

You could offer a framed A3 print, four mounted unframed shots, perhaps of smaller sizes, in one package. A second package may include two A3 framed prints and ten mounted prints of their choice and 50 postcards or greetings cards. You might include some decent passport photos without charge or offer a family photo book for an extra fee. You could offer a discount for a future shoot—perhaps baby on his/her first birthday, another shoot for when the 18 year old turns 21.

Clients may be a bit wary if an unknown person offers to take photographs in their home, so you could always suggest a local landmark or photogenic location, or even hire a studio or space for a few hours or half day.

There are numerous established portrait studios, many on high streets to raise their visibility and footfall, set up to take formal family portraits. Some offer a 'make-over' session by a makeup and hair stylist, alongside a photographic shoot. Some charge a fee; some offer a photo session for free with the hope of making money on the sale of prints.

A few portrait photographers also team up with other businesses, offering a complete package, perhaps with a beauty or hair salon. They are certainly good place to leave your promotional card or flier offering a set price deal. It could include a discount if they mention the salon.

There are also 'pop-up' studios, usually set up outside the shops in shopping malls, to catch passing trade. If you have portable lights and backdrops, contact your local council to find the contact name for the shopping mall or to ask about the possibilities of a pop-up studio in markets, malls, fetes, school fairs, etc.

Although a few studios still find a market with the formal style of almost Victorian portraits, many now offer more zany family shoots. Kids bouncing on trampolines, playing their musical instruments, chasing the family dog, creative collages of family members, unusual angles,—all studio shots and often with some computer trickery afterwards but bright, fun and modern. These shoots and subsequent sales of framed pictures can bring in a lot of money. One studio in London charges nearly £1000 for an hour's shoot, a set of prints and one large framed print. Studios that offer 'high society' portraits charge even more but often have a studio in the right postcode, with rent and rates that make your eyes water. See **Setting Up A Studio.**

Some photographers will also use their portrait shots to produce greetings cards and calendars for the clients. However, with the advent of online personalised card and calendar services, often at very low prices, this is not a lucrative line for most, unless you can get a commission from the Prime Minister and an order for his Christmas cards.

Many portrait photographers belong to the Society of Wedding & Portrait Photographers: *www.swpp.co.uk* or The Master Photographers' Association, *www.thempa.com*

Children

While wedding and portrait photographers will also photograph children: some specialise in portraits of just children. Certainly, there is a big market in more formal portraits of children, as although most parents have their own digital cameras, they will rarely achieve a photo worthy of framing on the wall.

Quite a few photographers have their own studios but as the fashion has turned away from more formal portraits to lively location shots, it is a low-overhead business to start. Marketing can be done by dropping fliers through doors, asking cafés, hair and beauty salons, children's toy and clothes shops to pin up your flier. Some advertise in free local magazines, such as London South West, the Families group of magazines and on websites such as School's Trader. Others use forums like Mumsnet to promote their services.

As children grow, this can be good repeat business. It can be worth offering a discount voucher for the next shoot, or for a recommendation, with the third party also receiving a discount.

Pets

A few photographers specialise in pet photography. Some may have their own studio, although it is unlikely that pet photography alone will bring in enough business to support it. What is more common is to see photographers to come to an arrangement with pet stores, or a pet store chain and set up a 'pop-up' studio within it. Some may rent studios in different areas for a day or two and door-drop fliers, pin notices in local parks etc., and perhaps advertise on local newspapers and in door-dropped free magazines.

There are also dog and cat clubs to market to, as well as breeder clubs, and of course, dog, cat and gerbil magazines. There are also plenty of shows where you can take a stand and market your services, perhaps offering a pet portrait there and then.

There are many tricks of the trade to photographing both pets and children, like blowing whistles to catch attention, etc. A local radio or TV station or publication may well be interested in hearing some of them and of past stories, good and bad. This would help generate interest.

Product & Packshots

It is not just the Argos catalogue that uses thousands of photographs. Every single product produced and almost every service offered needs photographs for brochures, publicity, packaging and websites.

Whatever product you are photographing, think creatively. Yes, follow the brief to get the right sort of image for its intended audience (reliable, tradition, fun, youthful, cool etc.,) but go beyond it. Many clients are business managers and, if you deal with them direct (as is often the case with smaller businesses), may have little imagination for the potential of their products. Even if the client wants extremely boring packshots, producing a second set of images in a new style may just educate them. They will hopefully be delighted. It could lead to a rethink on all their photography. If nothing else, they may well ask for prints for their reception area.

Most products are shot in a studio, and some photographers set up studios to do just that. Rates, either per shot, per hour, per half or full day, vary hugely but an internet search will give competitors' sites, some of which give their prices. London studios are invariably more expensive than those outside the capital. If you haven't got a studio, hire one by the day or half day. It will work out cheaper than renting full time. This cost must, of course, be priced into your estimate/fee. Find out if you have to pay extra for lights etc., or whether you are expected to bring your own.

Many studios offer 360 degree photography for the web where the product can 'spin', so customers can view it from every angle. Companies such as *www.swiftspin.co.uk* can do so using your photographs.

Studios usually also charge extra for cut-outs, retouching, CGI and prop sourcing. Top studios have their own stylists, or network of freelance stylists for food, hair etc. All packshot studios supply proofs, either in print or on computer.

PR Work

Public relations agencies and PR departments are there to promote their client/employer, to deal with press, trouble-shoot and ward off adverse publicity. Large companies may have in-house PR departments or use outside PR agencies, or a combination of the two. Almost every company, large or small, has a public relations contact on their website. It is they who often organise photography of portraits of clients and photographs of events and products. PR Week is the industry's trade magazine: *www.prweek. com* and see *http://toppragencies.prweek.co.uk* for a list of the Top 100 PR companies in the UK. Most of the big PR agencies are international. Also see the Public Relations Consultants Association *www.prca.org.uk*. Smaller PR agencies are listed in local directories.

Depending on the size of the client company and what they want, working for a PR company can be a very lucrative area of business. Even if you are fairly new to the profession, don't under-sell yourself. Sometimes clients have less confidence with someone 'cheap'

Marketing Photography

There is a fine, often indistinct, line between advertising agencies and marketing companies and some call themselves both. However, there are companies which do concentrate on marketing, be it in print or on the web. Some, including contract publishers, also call themselves marketing communications agencies (shortened to 'marcomms'), and produce marketing letters, fliers, newsletters, brochures, and magazines for clients. Some may call themselves direct marketing agencies or media agencies. They all need visual images.

There are also agencies and design companies producing 'below the line' promotional material, which includes packaging and point of sale material.

Larger companies invariably have a marketing department, although design and photography work for publications, for example, may be outsourced to a design agencies, another marketing company or an advertising agency but contacting the marketing department should point you in the right direction.

See:

The Chartered Institute of Marketing: www.cim.co.uk which also has a magazine; The Direct Marketing Association: www.dma-org.uk

The Marketing Society (www.marketing.society.org.uk).

The main trade magazine is *Marketing Week*, www.marketingweek. co.uk

Weddings

Weddings are the bread and butter for many photographers. There are an estimated 300,000 weddings and civil partnership ceremonies in the UK each year. Not all couples will hire photographers, of course,–some will rely on Uncle Ted with his compact camera. Budgets vary hugely, with some wedding photographers charging a mere £50 and providing, say, 10 prints and a disc of 20 shots, with the hope of selling more. Others offer a package which includes contact sheets, an album and a second album for the parents for £500-2000 and even more for society/celebrity weddings.

A web search will bring up competitors' sites that will show what they are charging. It does vary according to region.

The websites of wedding photographers are probably best kept to weddings, although you could also include Christenings, Anniversaries, etc. Keep your sales copy on your website (and brochure if you produce one), very clear as to exactly what is included in each package. Bride and bridegroom do not want an open-ended expense. For example:

Package A

Free consultation session

Free wedding venue pre-wedding visit

Free pre-wedding shoot

4 hours wedding day shoot

50–9 x 6 prints

2–12 x 10 prints

DVD of 200 images

Price £595.00

Or

Package D

Free consultation

Free wedding venue pre-wedding visit for two venues

Free pre-wedding shoot (one for bride, second photographer for groom)

12 hours shoot

Proof book

20–9 x 6 prints

50 page album, made by (name).

24 x 24 print on canvas

600 high-resolution images on disc

Free online gallery

Price: £1895.00

Four or five packages is usually enough—as long as they are clearly defined by what is on offer in each. More than that can cause confusion. If VAT registered, you must put whether the price includes VAT or be clear that VAT must be added. VAT will add 20% to your price, and price might be a determining factor in the choice of photographer.

Wedding photographers can add to their income by featuring a list of what else the couple could have, in addition to the package, and giving prices. Some photographers offer to produce 'thank you' cards with a photograph of the happy couple (this would apply equally to any other occasion where people receive gifts, such as anniversaries, birthdays, Christenings etc). Most suggest £1 a card, with usually a minimum order of 30-40 cards. Others offer extra mounted prints and canvas or acrylic mounted images, for an extra cost or a selection of photographs on a USB stick for use with a digital photoframe. Some offer an online gallery or website included it in a package price or as an extra charge.

Some wedding photographers also offer extra albums (usually of lesser quality than the main wedding album) for in-laws, best man and brides-maids. Some offer a little album or photobook, for an extra charge, for the couple to give as thank you gifts. Most will mention the brand of wedding album, praising its quality. Try and add value, which may appear a lot to the bride but which doesn't cost you much. It could be as simple as two free photo key rings with the best photo of the happy couple.

Wedding photographers charge a booking fee, often 10-25% of the total price, with the remainder payable four weeks before the wedding date. The booking fee deposit is invariably non-refundable and this should be stated as such in your terms and conditions page on your website and any paper-work/receipt/booking form.

Many photographers provide 'same day' services for proofs or even for an album of the formal pictures. They may then take orders for extra prints from guests at the reception. Some offer video (with sound) as well as stills photographs.

Wedding photographers often advertise in wedding magazines or attend/ take a stall at some of the many wedding shows that happen all over the country, usually in Spring. It is worth getting good quality postcards printed and asking if you can leave some in bridal gown shops, at registry offices, florists, hairdressers, suit hire companies etc.

These days, the bride and groom expect more than the formal portraits outside the church or registry office. They often also want the preparations photographed as well as the service, formal portraits, reception and guests. A female photographer might be a better bet for the bride's 'getting ready' scenes, and vice versa for the groom. A second photographer of the opposite sex may be in order. Ask the couple what suits them.

You cannot use any wedding photos for commercial use without permission and signed model releases. You may be able to sell photos of a celebrity wedding to a magazine or agency, so long as you were not trespassing.

If you are starting out, try searching for 'wedding photographer wanted' on local forums, Photoassist and Gumtree, where you may find jobs for assistants and second photographers. You will usually have to give away the rights to your work (other than for portfolio/marketing use) to the main photographer. Couples on a tight budget often advertise for a photographer on these sites, local forums and as well as on

www.craigslist.co.uk

www.preloved.co.uk

www.hitched.co.uk,

www.talkphotography.co.uk

www.confetti.co.uk

You can also list your services on:

www.weddingphotographerfinder.co.uk

www.ourweddingmemories.co.uk

www.mumsnet.com

www.netmums.com

www.schoolstrader.com

Some photographers find that, by just being around the registry office, (rarely the church), they pick up on-the-spot commissions.

Wedding photographers also need insurance: See **Insurance**

Society of Wedding and Portrait photographers: *www.swpp.co.uk*–runs annual trade events and offers advice. The Guild of Professional Photographers incorporates the Guild of Wedding Photographers, *www.photoguild. co.uk*

Being a member of a professional organisation can instil confidence in buyers if you feature it on your website and letterhead etc.

You can find good wedding albums, mounts or picture frames and digital frames at:

Folio Albums—www.folioalbums.com

Spicer Hallfield Ltd—www.spicerhallfield.co.uk

Denis Wright—www.denis-wright.com

Middlewall Album Company—www.middlewallalbumco.co.uk

Loxely Colour—http://loxelycolour.com

I Nobili—distributed by www.mapleframing.co.uk and www.photo-value.com, among others

GF Smith—wwgfsmithphotomount.co.uk

Mario Acerboni—www.italianweddingalbums.com.

Heritage—www.heritagephotoalbums.co.uk

Versatile Albums Ltd—www.versatilealbums.com

Somerset Albums—www.somersetalbums.com

Graphi Studio—www.graphistudio.com

Jorgensen—www.jorgensenalbums.com, distributed in the UK by www.swpm.net

Photovalue—www.photovalue.com

Aspinal of London—www.aspinaloflondon.com

Luminati Waycon Ltd—www.clear2c.co.uk (frames)

Crown Mounts—www.crownmounts.co.uk

Queensberry Albums—www.queensberryalbums.com New Zealand company, but with distributors in the UK

Ultimat—www.ultimatframes.com

Exclusive 7—www.exclusive7.com (digital frames)

Noble Macmillan—www.noblemacmillan.com

J Muir & Co Bookbinders—www.jmuirbookbinders.co.uk (bespoke albums and books)

Black Cat Bindery—www.blackcatbindery.com (bespoke albums)

Aerial Photography

As mentioned, the RAF is the obvious employer for those interested in aerial photography but there is a wider market.

Aerial photography is used in cartography (particularly in photogrammetric surveys which are often the basis for topographic maps), archaeology, movie production and location sourcing, environmental studies, surveillance, commercial advertising, conveyancing, town, road, rail and other land use project planning. Clients include architects, museums, production companies, Ordnance survey, councils, armed services, police, infrastructure and energy companies.

There are several agencies, photographers and stock libraries that specialise in aerial photography. Magazines often run picture essays of aerial shots. Some enterprising photographers will take aerial shots of homes and then try and sell prints. It is not essential to have a pilot's licence: it is difficult to fly a small plane and take photos at the same time.

Underwater Photography

Underwater photographers may also be marine biologists, or work for marine research institutes. While underwater photography does find markets as picture essays in magazines, stills have been somewhat surpassed by film. Several photographers have switched from stills to film. Film units may even have their own directors of underwater photography. There is still a market for underwater stills with stock libraries. Occasionally, there are underwater fashion and advertising shoots.

Some underwater photographers also become diving instructors, tourist guides or work for, or even set up, underwater photography schools in oceanside locations. There are also some forensic underwater photographers, called on by police forces and military. A few may find work for oil and minerals exploration companies, wreck explorers and even insurance companies. Most have Professional Association of Diving Instructors (PADI) qualifications.

Fine Art Photography

This is probably the hardest area of photography in which to make a living but photographers do gain recognition, often international and can be very successful. They have major (and minor) exhibitions, sell through specialist dealers and produce limited editions, one-offs, and fine art books of their work. They may achieve a following of collectors of their work.

All artists need to raise their profiles: talent apart, their prices are often reflected in their fame. Many artists use photography as a basis for their art work using collage or manipulation to make a unique piece. Some artists produce prints or limited edition prints which they sell at markets, fairs, arts festivals or sell rights to photographs to companies who produce fine art prints. You can also sell through online galleries—there are now galleries specialising in fine art photography, such as *www.troikaeditions.co.uk*, *www. milimgallery.com*, *www.contacteditons.co.uk*, *www.yellowkorner.com*, *www. novagallery.co.uk*, *www.eyestorm.com* and *www.20x200.com*. There are also craft ecommerce sites such as *www.etsy.com*. You can, of course, sell through your own ecommerce site but you should ensure you market it well and have the right SEO words so people can find it.

Many artists need funding, and they have different funding opportunities to, say, photojournalists. For most fine art funding and grant schemes, try:

www.artscouncil.org (for England)

www.artswales.org.uk

www.scottisharts.org.uk

www.artscouncil-ni.org.

The Arts Council also has a jobs site, www.artsjobs.org.uk, which occasionally runs ads for photographers or assistants.

Other useful sites include:

www.artquest.org.uk

www.artshub.co.uk

www.a-n.co.uk

www.artlyst.com

www.disabilityartsonline.org.uk

www.britishartists.co.uk

www.jotta.com

The Society for Artists lists many useful links: *www.saa.co.uk*. Your local council will also have a section on arts organisations in your area.

The above sites may also give you leads for studios or shared space although there are several organisation specialising in studio space, including

www.workspacegroup.co.uk and www.acme.org.uk.

Business Franchises

There are franchises in portrait, wedding, school and nursery, property and events photography. Most say they offer training and no experience is necessary, and some say a day or even a half a day's training will get you up and running.

Although franchises suit many people setting up their first business, and the franchise may offer information and support, it all comes at a cost, sometimes a very high cost. Some franchises offer 'exclusive territories' although how you persuade, say, all the event organisers in your territory that you and you alone can photograph their event is not explained.

The costs of photographic franchise vary hugely. One charges £17,900 franchise fee and then requires you to spend £30,000 (plus VAT) on equipment (presumably you have to buy from them, so they make even more) and buy its business management software as well. Others require an annual fee on top of a franchise licence fee. Some offer franchises for £9995, £2450 or as low as £699 for nursery photography, which includes a CRB check. Some will want a commission on your sales. The success of a franchise, like most businesses, depends on your ability to sell.

Some franchise sites claim you can earn £50,000 plus a year (although the small print says this is not guaranteed). If this were so, most photographers would be taking up franchises. Be very wary of unrealistic earnings potential.

For most photographers, a franchise makes little business sense. If you want to be an events photographer, there is nothing to stop you approaching event organisers, event management companies, or even your local football team. If you want to set up a studio for portrait work, the premises and equipment will cost you so much that there is unlikely to be much spare for a franchise license. While most claim that they also supply you with letterheads, marketing material, support, territories etc., you can probably do just as well by yourself.

Where To Find Work

www.arts.ac.uk/careers/opportunties. The website of the University of the Arts has a job board and although there for the benefit of its students and ex-students, there is no reason why other people cannot apply. A quick look in July revealed ads for freelance photographers to photograph handbags, fabric, fashion, a wedding and permanent jobs for two assistants, a photographic retoucher and in-house studio photographer.

www.bjp-online.com

www.creativepool.co.uk

www.artsjobs.org.uk (Arts Council)

www.creativematch.com

www.photoassist.co.uk

www.photographer.co.uk

www.professionalphotographer.co.uk

www.creativereview.co.uk

One-off jobs and 'assistant wanted' jobs are also often advertised on the following sites. They are usually more suited to students/beginners. You can usually search according to location and also post your services, but it is rarely worth paying for advertising.

www.craigslist.co.uk

www.gumtree.co.uk

www.movethat.co.uk

Most photography associations also have jobs boards.

It is never worth paying to join a job listing site. All they do is collate jobs advertised elsewhere. Any bona fide job should be free to view.

For journalist and PR jobs:

www.gorkana.com

www.theguardian.co.uk

For sports photography jobs

www.sportsjournalists.co.uk

For the charity sector,

www.charityjobs.co.uk

www.thethirdsector.co.uk

To find designers, writers, editors, etc also try:

www.linkedin.com

www.crowdspring.com

www.designcrowd.com

www.99designs.com

To bid on freelance jobs (or advertising for writers, editors etc):

www.freelancer.com

www.elance.com

www.odesk.com

www.vworker.com

www.guru.com

www.scriptlance.com

www.peopleperhour.com

For the USA,

www.freelancephotojobs.com

www.photoassistant.com

www.photographersjobs.com

www.mediabistro.com

www.krop.com

www.talent200.com

There are several websites that collate all the jobs boards. Try

www.indeed.co.uk

www.totaljobs.com

www.simplehired.co.uk

www.jobrapido.co.uk

You could also try the sites of photography studios, stock libraries, agencies and groups of photographers, as they may not advertise with recruitment agencies.

Magazines also have jobs boards: *Creative Review, Campaign, UK Press Gazette, Media Week.* Jobs also occasionally appeared on sites like BAPLA, AoP, ArtsHub and ArtQuest.

Chapter Three

The Photographer and Other Work

Νew photographers need to start somewhere: established photographers may need to expand their work options. Few photographers are fortunate to be paid well enough just to take photographs and many need another string to their bow. Listed here are some other options in related fields.

Photographers' Assistant

The obvious starting point for most photographers is as a photographer's assistant. This can be permanent, part-time or freelance. A photographer's assistant ensures the smooth running of a shoot. It means carrying equipment, retouching and captioning images, organising props, looking after clients and models, down to sweeping the floor and making tea. The best photographers' assistants are flexible and not too proud to do menial tasks. It is also their job to anticipate what the photographer wants and to make the photographer look good to clients. They can learn a great deal from working alongside a professional.

Assistant photographer jobs can be found on

www.photoassist.co.uk

www.photographers.co.uk

www.bjp-online.com

and the generic jobs board sites mentioned above. You can also write to established photographers, although it's a bit of a shot in the dark. Even a tenuous connection, such as being a follower on Twitter or Facebook, that you saw their work in X book or at Y exhibition, that your aunt once had tea with their mother, helps. Always address letters and emails by name, not Dear Sir or Madam. Some photographers occasionally offer work experience, which may just lead to an assistant's job.

Second Photographer

Sometimes shoots require a second photographer. This is especially true of wedding photography, where the main photographer takes the formal shots and the second photographer captures more informal shots of guests. Event and sport photographers also often use second photographers as they cannot be everywhere at once. The above websites, photo forums, Gumtree and Facebook can often throw up calls for a second photographer.

Digital Imagery Work

Some photographers also become specialists in digital asset management and image editing, using the most sophisticated software. They may work freelance or for media agencies and publishers. The potential employment (and employability) for IT work as a second string goes way beyond just retouching the model's eyebrows. There are numerous companies offering digital photographic editing, manipulation and stop-motion, which may advertise for technicians. Press agencies, TV and publishers all use experts who can handle software for digital photography. Newspapers may also want specialists. There are also ads for teachers of specific software, as well as jobs for technicians, within companies, colleges and schools.

There are also 'Teching' jobs—someone who accompanies a photographer and using a laptop, transmits the photographs almost as soon as the photographer takes them (particularly with events and sports work. Agencies and newspapers photographers and some freelancers use them. Some people, either in a company or as a freelance, also offer services to download photos to stock libraries.

Darkroom

Although most photographers use digital cameras these days, there is still a demand for people and studios that produce quality prints from black and white film. There are, for example, several studios and people with their own darkrooms that make a living producing black and white prints for others, although some excellent studios have gone bust in recent years. Those that do survive will usually also develop colour and make colour prints, as well as print from large format cameras. Many will advertise jobs within photographic magazines, *Creative Review* or on sites like *www.photographers.co.uk*.

Photographic Libraries

Some photographers set up their own stock photo libraries, perhaps inviting others to put their work with them. Others work for stock libraries as picture editors, researchers, managers or in sales. Jobs for picture managers/researchers for picture libraries are often advertised on *The Guardian* jobs website.

Agencies

Some photographers work for, or even set up, their own photo agency. It may be just one photographer, or several, who shoot a particular subject or in a specified geographic area. They shoot photos that are used by news media or for fillers. They, or a manager, will sell them to the press.

Picture Desk Assistant

Often working in magazines, newspapers, TV and for web companies, a picture desk assistant helps the picture editor. They help organise the logistics of a shoot, chase commissioned pictures, handle buying pictures and negotiating rights, picture research, captioning, administration and office support. They may need to use photo-editing software.

Picture Researcher

Picture researchers source images (including photographs, photographs of art, old photographs, old documents, etc.,) from all types of places, from stock libraries and museums to private collections, galleries and individuals. They research and source images to a brief, finding the correct images for a company, newspaper, magazine, book publisher, and stills for TV and film. Many picture researchers are freelance, commissioned to work on a specific project, such as a book for a publishing company. Big book, magazine and newspaper publishers and stock libraries have their own picture researchers.

Picture researchers have to clear and negotiate rights on behalf of the publisher, within the budget they have been given. They may have to write captions, or at least find information to enable a writer or sub-editor to do so. They also have to supply correct credit information for use alongside the image in a publication.

Stock libraries also have picture researchers—if a client wants to see photographs of a specific subject, they will search their files for a selection. However, with the use of the internet, most libraries are searchable online.

Picture researchers have their own society: *www.picture-research.org.uk*. The site also has a list of photographic collections and libraries. See also The British Association of Picture Libraries and Agencies, *www.bapla.org.uk*, which organises the annual BAPLA Picture Buyers Fair, which many picture researchers attend. There are also several Expos in America, usually New York and Chicago, attended by picture buyers.

In the USA, many belong to the American Society of Picture Professionals: *www.aspp.com*.

There are training courses in picture research. Popular ones are held at the London College of Communications, The Publishing Training Centre and the London School of Publishing.

Picture Editor

Picture editors usually work in book, newspaper or magazine publishing. They commission photographers to illustrate an article or book. Their pool of photographers may be staff or freelance, or both. While they often have a stable of photographers they use on a regular basis, most are open to seeing and using new photographers to keep their publication looking creative and fresh and to finding amazing new talent.

The picture editor makes the final selection, often with the art director, of which photos will be used and how. They also make the final selection from the material a picture researcher has found or instruct their assistant or picture researcher to find more/different images.

Their work invariably includes drawing up contracts with the photographers (or picture libraries) and negotiating fees for the shoot and the usage rights they need. They have briefs from their editors to meet, from which they must then brief the photographer. They are responsible for meeting deadlines, will have budgets to adhere to and may well negotiate syndication, although the bigger media outlets have syndication departments. Most picture editors on national newspapers are also photographers. They also have their own association: see *www.piced.net*. Many in the press belong to the National Union of Journalists.

Art Director

Although usually trained in graphic design, an art director can come from a variety of backgrounds, including photography, often advertising, fashion or editorial. They will commission freelancers or set a brief for their in-house photographers, illustrators and graphic and typography designers. They are similar to picture editors, in that they will invariably edit shoots and make the final selection and creative decisions. Most art directors (sometimes called Creative Directors) and art buyers will read *Campaign* and *Creative Review*, where jobs are also advertised.

Art Buyer

An art buyer commissions photographers and illustrators, sometimes under the watchful eye of the art director. They may also be responsible for buying stock pictures, which they research or they may have a picture researcher. They are more common in the advertising industry.

Gallery and Museum Work

Some photographers work in a gallery, as a curator or exhibitions manager, or even as gallery owner. Many museums and galleries have their own photographers or use freelancers to catalogue work, to supply photographs for their own and third-party publications and to produce postcards, greetings cards and posters for the gallery or museum shop.

Picture Managers/Sales

Agencies and stock libraries are in the business of selling photographs and need people to recognise the value of photos in their stock libraries, whether for press or editorial use and syndication. They can see the commercial value of photographs and know where and how to sell them. They have good contacts with picture desks, not just for news photos but for timely fillers.

Syndication Managers

Press agencies, most stock libraries and newspapers will have syndication departments to exploit the sales of the photographs they have. It may be they syndicate staff work or freelance work or sell prints from past issues of the newspaper. They will be adept at negotiating rates, have an amazing contacts database of outlets and are able to act quickly. They ensure they have the right captions and credits, and monitor sales and payments from clients as well as paying fees to photographers.

Television

Occasionally, there will be a TV series with a professional photographer teaching young photographers, setting briefs and then talking about the results. Although the TV production companies tend towards big names (Martin Parr, Rankin, etc.,), a few lesser known photographers have made it onto the small screen. The BBC's *Countryfile* programme, for instance, has an occasional feature with a photographer giving tips. Wildlife programmes sometimes do the same.

Although it is very difficult to get a series, even if you are a well-known, established photographer, your local television company might just be interested in one-off or regular small feature, for inclusion in another programme, especially if the programme is running a photographic competition. To see BBC regional television programmes, *www.bbc.co.uk*. For other production companies, see **Unit Stills Photographer**.

Television is highly competitive and can be quite cut-throat: there has been more than one instance of a photographer approaching a producer with a programme or feature idea, only to find the producer takes the idea and uses his or her favoured photographer.

Teaching

The expansion of photography courses at CGSE, A level, BTEC, City and Guilds, and degree and postgraduate level at schools, colleges and universities across the UK means there is great demand for photography tutors. Many private companies also offer photography courses, held across the UK and abroad. But equally, such jobs are very popular, especially when so many great photographers simply cannot make a good living within their chosen field and need the regular income from teaching. Not all tutors are full-time. Many colleges and universities, for example, have visiting or part-time lecturers. Private courses may only require tutors at weekends or evenings.

To find teaching jobs visit

www.guardian.co.uk

www.talent.ac.uk

www.bjp-online.com

The Times Educational Supplement and *The Times Higher Educational Supplement* also advertise teaching posts,

Teaching–Further Education

To teach in a further education (FE) college, employers are likely to require significant experience or a degree in the relevant subject, and may also require tutors to have a teaching qualification or take one within the first couple of years of employment.

Teaching–Higher Education

Most employers require tutors to have a degree in the appropriate subject and possibly a teaching qualification. However, there are some excellent professional photographers teaching in Higher Education, either permanently or as a visiting lecturer, without formal qualifications. Colleges and universities teaching photography degree courses can be more flexible about qualifications than schools—your portfolio, achievements, reputation and personality will often be more valuable than a degree. However, it is most likely that you will be expected to gain a teaching qualification while in the post.

Private courses

Most private schools and colleges do not oblige tutors to have a formal teaching qualification. If you teach under-18s or vulnerable people, the school/college will apply for a Criminal Records Bureau (CRB) check.

If a school, including boarding, state and private (public) schools, doesn't already offer any photography course, you could draw up a business plan for a photography course, after-school club or summer school activity for which the school and/or pupils pay. You should send it, with a covering letter, to the Head of School. It is important to check out the minimum ratio of students to tutors they require—it may mean finding some additional tutors.

There are private photography courses run across the UK. They often have their own premises. Many of these organisations are set up as 'not-for-profit' (a form of charitable status). They are required to run the organisation as a commercial business and after expenses, to plough profits back into the business and meet its stated community aims. They may well be able to offer part-time tutoring work but it pays to be flexible, as many courses will run in the evening or at weekends. If you want to set up a not-for-profit photography venture as a business, the Charities Commission has full details of how to do so.

It may even be worthwhile starting a photographic course as a straight business venture, although you will face stiff competition from established colleges, universities and private courses and even camera clubs.

Research what is already on offer in your area and whether there are already camera clubs and courses. Local forums and amateur photography forums will give you an idea of the numbers of photographers, both professional and amateur, in your area and maybe start small by offering short courses at first. You might team up with a local gallery, local library, café or even pub, where you use their premises for a small fee or even for free.

Tour Guides, Holidays and One-To-One Tutoring

Some enterprising photographers offer to act as guide/tutors on personal tours for groups or even one-to-one. Some also offer one-to-one photographic tuition. They advertise on Facebook, Flickr, Lonely Planet, Craigslist, Gumtree and local and photographic forums.

Many photographers also offer courses (often as short holidays) at their homes, arranging to accommodate and cater for photographers or to put them up in a local B&B or hotel. If you have the space or a good local B&B/ hotel and are in an area that could be a popular photographic holiday destination, in the UK or abroad, this can be a good opportunity for earning. You will need public liability insurance, especially if you have the public coming to your home or premises, even if you rent short-term. You should also tell your home insurance company and mortgage lender if you intend to use your home for business.

Another option is to set up a travel company and sell photographic holidays, perhaps escorting a group to the destination. This requires a lot of organisation—if you offer a full package, you will be responsible for flights, hotels or villa rentals, transport and maybe even food. If you want to go this route, it would be wise to set up a limit company, so if things go wrong, your personal liability is limited. See *www.businesslink.gov.uk*.

If you haven't run a business before, and are a bit daunted by the prospect of a full-blown travel business, you could approach specialist companies that already run photographic holidays (most have a Facebook page) and offer your services as a tutor/guide.

Other companies offer activity holidays, for instance, painting or hiking. If they do not already have a photographic holiday, you might suggest a possible itinerary, and why you would make a good tutor/guide. You will need a comprehensive marketing and business plan.

You can find the contact details of most tour operators at The World Travel Marketing annual exhibition and its website has a list of exhibitors and associations: *www.wtmlondon.com*. ABTA, which represents most holiday companies, also has a list of members and non-members. It does cost to access them, so WTM might be initially a better option.

Chapter Four

It's Not What You Know...

Some fields of photography can be pretty solitary but it doesn't matter in which field of photography you specialise, you need contacts. Recommendation is the best marketing tool but a simple referral can open doors, so networking is as important for marketing as your website and card.

Buying a list of contacts is not networking. Interacting online can be but meeting people, however briefly, and establishing a relationship certainly is. Pretty soon you have a network. The more people you meet, the better. For every person you meet, they know a whole lot of other people. Tenuous maybe, but a great many jobs come through referrals.

One of the reasons for the success of web based organisations like LinkedIn (over 100 million members) is that everyone recognises the benefits of networking. There is more than a bit of truth in the saying: 'it's not what you know, but who you know.'

On a social, and increasingly business, level we see the phenomenal success of Facebook and Twitter and more recently, Google+. People want to make connections. Photographers use social media to connect and market themselves: they join groups within networks, not just those of other photographers but of the industries in which they work. Whatever field you work in, there will a group for you. If you are female, there are even groups within groups, just for you. Women in property and women in construction groups on LinkedIn are just two that spring to mind.

Networking is not just a case of going to an event, working the room, handing out your business card and giving the hard sell. It is about creating a relationship, one that could be of mutual benefit. Always determine what you can offer as much as what you will get out of meeting. It's a two-way street: appear too selfish, too concerned with getting work for yourself, and you could get the cold shoulder. Offer encouragement and advice, if you can, and refer them to others who may be interested in their service/product and they just might do the same for you.

As well as online networks, there are network clubs for all sorts of groups. Some networks charge (and are businesses in their own right), some are informal or local groups. It is tempting to go solely for groups of other photographers so you can meet and moan, celebrate, etc. While meeting other photographers is important (see below), as far as networking for work contacts is concerned, meeting diverse groups of professional people is a better bet.

Not every photographer likes the networking side of the business (an amazing number of photographers are shy) but you really have to get over it. You don't have to be the life and soul of the party but don't be the wallflower either. If meeting someone for the first time, ask about them rather than talk about yourself. There is a very good, very readable book, *The Network Effect*, by Tony Newton and Judy Perle, (published by Management Advantage, price £8.99). It takes you through everything you need to know about connecting to other people with lots of practical advice and case studies. If you are not good at networking, do read it.

If you make contacts, don't let them slip away. A follow up email or postcard saying how nice it was to meet them is enough. It is not a hard sell but it does help maintain the relationship. If someone emails or calls regarding a possible job, respond as soon as you can. In this age of instant communication, if they cannot get hold of you, or you don't call back until the next day, don't be surprised if they go elsewhere. Even if you are up a mountain somewhere and cannot possible get back to do a job, reply and tell them so and when you will be available. Not replying at all will probably get you struck off their list of photographers.

Keep Your Name in the Buyer's Mind

One picture editor said she gets postcards from one of her stable of photographers from wherever he is in the world, even if not working for her. He doesn't say anything about work or future work but just comments on the weather, the food, the sites, the people. She really looks forward to them—and always, always says yes to seeing him when he calls with a photo story to sell. Another places value on Christmas Cards—he has quite a collection of amazing images and always remembers who bothered to send him one. One company director has his office lined with framed photos of extraordinary landscapes, sent every year from the photographer he now always uses to take pictures of his hotels.

Although no-one should go over the top with presents (it reeks of a kind of bribery), photographers should try and maintain contacts, even by sending a postcard/Christmas card now and then.

On the other side of the coin is the story of one picture editor who thought he'd become great friends with a photographer he used a lot. With their respective spouses, they dined at each other houses: they went to the cinema and theatre together. Then the picture editor resigned, to do something entirely different. The photographer never contacted him again. 'I was evidently no longer useful, I suppose'. Very foolish, as within a year, the picture editor was back in charge of a picture desk. Needless to say, he never used that photographer again, and picture editors do talk to each other.

Getting Feedback

Every photographer could benefit from comparing their work to that of others, and getting some feedback. This is especially true for young photographers who may have been praised to the sky, perhaps by family and friends but reality hits when they enter the real world. Picture editors often bemoan the fact that some photographers think they are better than they are.

No photographer should work in isolation. Feedback, whether positive or negative, is essential. One of the many values of a photography degree course is the time to experiment, to find your own voice and get criticism, good or bad, from tutors and peer groups.

It is said that limitation is the springboard of inspiration, so if you have yet to be commissioned, you might set yourself a brief. Many books are available that set photo projects. Most quality national newspapers (usually online only) and competitions set photographic briefs. Then get the work critiqued. Many professional associations, galleries and photographic festivals run portfolio reviews and mentoring schemes. There are also plenty of meet-up groups and even camera clubs (often scorned by professionals) where you can get feedback and learn. Take advantage–you might not always like what you hear but if you can't take some criticism and rejection, you shouldn't be in this industry. Look at the present top photographers in fields of work in which you are interested and aim to match that level, not only technically but in concept.

Photographers continue learning and honing their craft: the lensmen who had to relearn digital: the photographers who obsessively photograph the same thing again and again until they are satisfied. You also have to keep abreast of each generation of software. There are internet-based storage and transfer systems to master. New styles of photography means you need to keep up with what's current, what's popular. New cameras are produced with alarming frequency that can do new and amazing things. Press photographers now have to learn to take high definition video—there is a lot to keep pace with in our digital world. But you shouldn't get carried away with gadgetry. Some of the most iconic photographs were taken on plate cameras and Box Brownies.

All photographers need encouragement to keep shooting and to make today's work better than yesterday's. As Samuel Beckett said: 'Fail. Try again. Fail better'.

Mentors

Many photographers have learnt their trade by being taught and nurtured by mentors. Most photographers will acknowledge their success in part to the generosity of an established photographer. It can be worthwhile making contact with a photographer whose work you admire and/or works in a similar field to yourself and ask if they could meet you to talk for an hour.

Do tell them why you have chosen them to approach, otherwise it sounds like you picked them at random. It can also help to have specific questions you'd like to ask, technical or business, rather than say you like to 'talk photography'. You might be offered a chance to attend a shoot, where you can learn a great deal just by watching and listening. Just make sure it's at their convenience. Suggest coffee or lunch and pay the bill.

Of course, photographers won't appreciate it if you try and muscle in on their market and clients but on the whole, established photographers are pretty confident people who may well enjoy having their own protégé. You may, of course, get no response or even rejection but rejection is part and parcel of being a photographer. Pick yourself up and try elsewhere. You could also ask all your family and friends if they know a professional photographer. That tenuous link may be all it takes to open the door.

Some professional photographers' associations, like SWPP, *www.swpp.com*, run mentor schemes

Photographers are also generous in sharing their technical knowledge. Many write blogs. Ken Rockwell (*www.kenrockwell.com*) is one of the best known.

Gear, wheels and raring to go

Being a freelance photographer means you have to supply all your own camera gear. Buy the best you can afford—consider it an investment. Quality shows. Most professional photographers have top end dslrs and lenses by Nikon or Canon.

You will probably be expected to have your own transport too. Unless you can afford a driver, a full driving license and owning or hiring a car or bike is prerequisite for many jobs.

Always be ready to go–keep your passport up-to-date.

Joining a Professional Association

There are associations for almost every field of photography and joining one can bring many benefits. Certainly, membership does cost but what you often get in return can be very good value for money. The prestige of those letters after your name can help instil confidence in you, especially if mentioned on your website. Most associations run social events, training, seminars, workshops, portfolio reviews, and offer legal and technical advice, magazines, bursaries, awards and competitions, forums, exhibitions and often, lower insurance rates that the association can negotiate on behalf of its members. Some association sites carry jobs adverts; membership of some will also qualify you for a press card.

The main ones are:

> The Association of Photographers: (www.the-aop.org.uk)
>
> The Royal Photographic Society: www.rps.org
>
> The British Institute of Professional Photographers: www.bipp.com
>
> The British Press Photographers' Association: www.thebppa.com
>
> Editorial Photographers UK and Ireland: www.epuk.org
>
> The National Union of Journalists: www.nuj.org.uk
>
> The Bureau of Freelance Photographers: www.thebfp.com
>
> The Chartered Institute of Journalists: www.cioj.co.uk
>
> The Master Photographers' Association: www.thempa.com
>
> The Society of Wedding & Portrait Photographers: www.swpp.co.uk (affiliated to many other smaller specialist associations)
>
> The Guild of Photographers: www.photoguild.co.uk

There are other smaller societies and associations and your decision to join will depend on several factors: whether you need membership to be eligible for a press card, the field of photography, what you want from joining an association, what it offers for the membership fee (free legal advice, for example, is one valuable benefit) and of course, your budget. Most quote lower rates for students and some offer lower rates for overseas members or associate membership.

Chapter Five

Marketing

Websites

Prerequisite to getting known and getting work is a website, with right key words that will get you to the top of the list on search engines like Google.

Register a domain name, your URL website name, so you can include it on business cards and letterheads.

There are thousands of companies where you can register a name—each with its own pricing structure. Popular ones include *www.123-reg.co.uk*, *www.names.co.uk*, *www.godaddy.com*, *www.ukreg.com*, *www.fasthosts.co.uk* and *www.hostgater.com*—an internet search will bring up many more. You can use their search facilities to type in your chosen domain name and see if it is available with the ending you want (such as .com or .co.uk). Other endings are on offer, from .info to .net. Most of the companies selling domain names offer to host your site as well.

The costs depend on the popularity of your chosen URL domain name: they range from a few pounds a year to hundreds. Some offer cheaper fees for a two year period but almost all companies will raise the fees on renewal. Forget to renew (though the company should remind you when it is due for renewal) and the name goes back on the market.

Some web designers/web building companies will offer to register a name for you, often for free as part of the design package. However, it is always advisable to buy your own domain name.

What's in a Name?

Names matter—easy to pronounce, easy to spell, easy to remember and an indication that you are a photographer all seem obvious, but we are not all sensible when it comes to names for businesses.

When thinking of your business name, even as a freelancer, make sure your chosen name is not already taken by a company. You can search the names of UK companies on the Companies House website, www.companieshouse. gov.uk and The Intellectual Property Office, www.ipo.gov.uk, which gives trade mark details. You can, as a sole trader, trade under any name you like, so long as it is not infringing the rights of anyone else, is not passing yourself off as something or someone else or could cause confusion.

You should also try searching on the net using your desired name as there may be, here or abroad, a freelance photographer, studio or photo company with a similar name. They may be .com or .net while the domain name you want is .co.uk but such confusion is best avoided.

It is unwise to use the word 'King' or 'Queen' (you have to get special permission to use some words) or to use 'International', especially if you have limited company status, to make yourself sound a bigger business than you are.

For most freelancers, some variation of their own name is usual. Before you decide and get letter heads printed and spend money registering a domain name, think about whether you want to be known as, say, a sports photographer by using 'sports' in the name. It might limit your work options.

There are several sites, including *www.businessnamegeneration.com www. namegenerator.co.uk* and *www.companynamegenerator.co.uk*, where you can enter a word and the site searches all the possible variations of company, trading and domain names and whether the domain name has been taken. On the whole it is better that your trading and domain name does what it says on the tin.

Make it Memorable

If your name is Ilyanovitch Stanivsaliski, do think about making it shorter, more accessible, easy to pronounce, memorable and not prone to typographical mistakes. www.yanophoto.com for example, is better than Ily_S_photography1.com. Names are better remembered than numbers and initials. Having the word 'photo', photography or 'photographer' in the domain name will also help identify you as a photographer.

> Keep it simple
>
> Make it memorable
>
> Try not to use dots or dashes or underlines

Include the word photo or photographer or photography (unless you are Rankin, when you can just put Rankin).

Type out your chosen name before you buy. Words run together can take on an altogether new meaning, called Slurls (think Experts Exchange, Pen Island, Therapist Finder).

It is debatable whether you should go for .com, .co.uk, .eu or .net but by specifying .co.uk, you at least locate yourself somewhere. It is reported that people trust sites more if they know where they are based. You can of course buy .co.uk and .com (and any other ending), and when someone enters the address, they are automatically pointed to your main site.

You will also need a company to host your site. It could be the company from which you bought your domain name, your internet service provider (although the free space is usually limited), your web designer or one of the web building companies.

Website Design

Every website should have a home page. Don't be tempted to have some fancy flash graphics which then need a 'click here to enter site'. People want to get to your pictures as fast as possible. It is also very unwise to force people to register and need a password to log on before they can view your photographs. The rule for web design is 'don't make me think'.

Many picture buyers advise against flash, music or pdf downloads. A gallery that people can easily see, perhaps with an arrow to the next photograph in that category is a good idea. Look at many other photographers' sites to see what looks good, is easy to use and use one as your basis to brief a designer.

Remember KISS—keep it simple, stupid.

A home page should give a bit about yourself, preferably with a self-portrait (instilling confidence in the viewer that you are real). If you have won any awards/competitions, published any books and/or have an impressive list of clients, mention them.

You should also, of course, give your telephone numbers (a landline and mobile). Landlines are important—many people do not want the expense of phoning a mobile, especially if you are in Nepal at the time. Make it easy for overseas visitors to call you by including the international dialling code (+44 for Britain).

For security and marketing reasons, many photographers do not put where they are based but it can be advisable to give a general address of town, county and country, without giving your actual house number/street address. If you have a studio for portraits, product shots etc., then an address is important and it should also appear on Google maps and local listings.

Your email should be on every page, with a call to action (such as 'contact me'). You could integrate your email, so if they click your email address, their own email opens immediately with your address in the TO: line. You could also have a form where people can contact you through the site.

Limited companies in the UK must, by law, also give a postal address on their website but this can be the registered office (often your accountant's address), rather than your own.

A Simple Gallery

Unless you are adept at web design and html, you will either have to use an off-the-peg web builder or employ a web designer.

If you want to simply have your photos in a gallery on the net, you can use a photo sharing site. However, nothing beats having your own site for a professional look. Photo sharing sites include:

www.flickr.com

www.photobucket.com

www.picassa.com

www.expono.com

www.snapshack.net

www.smugmug.com

www.facebook.com

http://photie.com

www.personalgrid.com

http://tinyalbum.com

www.zoomorama.com

http://72photos.com

http://drop.io (bought by Facebook)

www.imageloop.com

www.shareapic.net

www.dphoto.com

www.bayimg.com

www.imagehost.ro

www.deviantart.com

www.Mpix.com

www.Photostore.com

Off-The-Peg

You can get free off-the-peg solutions, where you have a choice of ready-made templates into which you upload your photographs and text. Thousands of companies offer such services, including Microsoft Office Live Small Business, WordPress, Weebly, Yola, Webs.com, and Wix. Google, in association with the government and Yola, offers Getting British Business Online, www.gbbo.co.uk, with domain name, website, email and support, all free for a year. Many web hosting sites also offer web site builders. Use of a website builder, domain name, and hosting your site can cost as little as £5 a month.

Whether you go for a free offer or pay more for more space, ensure you have a good bandwidth to ensure speedy download of images. Avoid any freebie website builder that has pop-up adverts which appear on your site—they irritate clients no end. Free site hosting may also mean your URL (your website name) has the host's or web-builder's name in the address (www.yourname. theirname.com). It doesn't look as professional, nor is it as memorable, as having just your website name (www.yourname.com). Most allow you to have just your own domain name, for a fee.

Photographers tend towards companies that are familiar with photographers and understand that photo quality and download speeds are important. Popular sites include:

>www.clikpic.com
>
>www.photium.com
>
>www.photoshelter.com
>
>www.photogalaxy.co.uk
>
>www.allwebcodesign.com
>
>www.zenfolio.com
>
>www.photographers-portfolio.co.uk
>
>www.amazinginternet.com

All have a range of paid-for packages, from around £30-60 a year up to c.£200 a year for 2000 pictures. Most offer built in watermark services and a range of templates from which to choose and a number of email addresses. All these companies will host and manage your site for you on their servers. You do not need knowledge of web development to use them.

Customised websites

You can, of course, go the fully customised route and use a web designer. Web designers for photography sites are also listed on photography associations' websites, such as the Association of Photography. You can also find thousands of web designers on the net or you could invite designers to bid on *www.freelancer.com*, *www.elance.com* and *www.peopleperhour.com*. Expect a lot of responses from all over the world, so make sure you see examples of their work and that they are willing to supply references. Pay by PayPal or WorldPay, or credit card, never debit card. Never give out your bank details.

If you opt for a web designer, be clear about what you want and what is—and is not—included in the price and get at least three quotes. It should not cost you more than the top of the range off-the-peg sites. Ask what happens if you want to add extra images and pages, change and add words, add an ecommerce facility or integrate a blog. How much will they charge? What happens if you want to move to another hosting site—who owns your domain name? If you want to move lock, stock and barrel, do you have to start again? It doesn't really matter where the web designer is based, although you might be a bit circumspect about cheap offers from some countries.

Your website should be clear, both in design and the message you are giving. Keep each page design consistent with the other pages, so viewers know they are on the same site. Many people don't like sites with white type out of a black or colour background, as they are harder to read. Similarly, if the design is confusing, with fancy borders, different typefaces and too many little bits of information all over the place, it can be a turn-off.

Links

Web experts often suggest having reciprocal links of other services and products on your site. This can bring you traffic from other sites but there is also the danger of people clicking on a link and moving away from your site. Try instead to leave comments on blogs, forums and newsgroups, giving a link to your own website address if possible. If website addresses and links are not allowed, adding 'Your name, photographer', is better than a tag like 'lens-fiend' if people want to follow up and look at your site.

Words Matter

You may be a visual person but it cannot be stressed enough that you need Search Engine Optimisation (SEO)—that is, using the key words people use to search for what they want. To stand any chance of being found and on or near page one when someone uses a search engine, think about what you offer and what words people would use to search. For instance 'Press Photographer in Newcastle', 'wedding photographer Huddersfield'. Most people never look beyond the second or third page of search results, so getting high on search rankings, preferably on page one, is important.

You can find which key words are most searched for by visiting the websites of search engines, such as Google and Yahoo!, or specialist services such as WordTracker, Keyword Discovery, Overture or Wordze. Most offer a limited service for free, which is usually enough to understand the terms people use when searching.

Even if you use the right words, it can take several weeks to climb the ranks of search engines.

Make sure key words are repeated on each web page. Don't overdo it so it doesn't make sense or just looks like a list of words—it can backfire as search engines may flag this up as over promotion and you may well be penalised. Caption your pictures as well, so they come up in both web and image searches, especially if you can include SEO words. 'Photograph at sunset of springer spaniel dogs racing the waves on the beach at Brighton' is better than 'Alfie and Chocky having fun'. Blog pictures should also have captions for the same reason.

200-250 words of text per page plus headings on every page should suffice, using the right key words where possible. Whether you write the copy yourself or pay someone to do it for you, proof read it many times and ask family/friends to proof read it as well. Bad grammar and spelling put people off very quickly. A blog as part of your site, which you update regularly, can also help raise your site in search engine listings.

If you are looking for a writer, try posting an advert on a local forum or on www.*freelancer.co.uk* or www.*peopleperhour.co.uk* and inviting bids. If you are British, ask for English as a first language. Remember that writers from the USA spell, for example, colour as color. Professional writers should produce copy to the right length, with essential key words (tell them what they are), with excellent grammar and no spelling mistakes.

You could also ask for a bid to translate your text into one or more language. This is useful if you hope for work from abroad but you should make it clear whether you speak the language—don't mislead. Most websites with more than one language have country flag icons that can be clicked on to bring up text in that country's language.

Photographic Resolution for the Web

Photographs need not be high resolution for websites—72dpi is fine and they are unlikely to be 'stolen' at that dpi. If the photographs are too large, they may take ages to download. It is said that if a web-page takes more than eight seconds to load, people lose interest.

Watermark your images

If you sell your pictures over the net, and want to display better quality at a larger size, do watermark your pictures. Once you have made a sale, you can allow the client to access the higher resolution photos without the watermark.

You need a watermark utility such as Adobe Photoshop and utilities such as PicMarkr, Watermark.ws. Visual Watermark, Watermark Studio, uMark, Watermark Software. Most web building companies offer watermarks. Stock libraries will watermark your images with their name.

You can use the watermark as another form of marketing, putting

©www.yourname.com. Some photographers see watermarks as distractions, but done subtly, they can look fine and help protect your work. Of course, anyone really intent of stealing your photograph can remove the watermark using software, but it can help deter people.

Selecting Photographs for Websites

Show only your very best photographs. While first impressions count, not everyone will land on your homepage when searching. Every photo should be as great as the next.

If you shoot a lot of different subjects, categorise them, (landscapes, wildlife, urban landscapes etc). If you have several categories, about ten shots per category is enough. Having said that, the websites that work best as marketing tools often show work in one field only, one of your areas of specialisation, like sports or architecture. Some photographers will have three or four websites, each dedicated to one field.

Your work might sit quite happily on the same site—landscapes and wildlife categories, for example, but sports with fashion or architectural photos with glamour don't go together, and can lead the viewer away from your site towards a specialist.

It is easier to publicise yourself if you are a specialist, although you can, of course, specialise in several areas but don't say you can shoot anything. Jacks-of-all- trades get less work.

Advertising Your Prices

Whether you mention prices depends on your intended market. If you are using ecommerce to sell prints, you should, of course, feature the price per size, perhaps charging extra for mounts or frames and postage and packing. (Remember to add VAT if you are VAT registered: retail prices should be displayed to include the VAT).

If you take product shots or portraits you might wish to put on 'prices from…' on your website, cards and other promotional material, although people like an idea of a fixed fee, rather than an open-ended one or 'contact me for a quote'. You might offer a package, such as 'Three professional pack shots for just…'

If you are looking for editorial, fashion, corporate or advertising commissions, it is not advisable to put indications of prices on your website as you could easily over—or under–price yourself.

Getting Your Website Known

It is obviously vital your website is submitted to search engines but you can also submit your site address to many free internet directories. If your work is primarily local (such as events photography) then list it on local directories, and *places.google.com/business*, *local.yahoo.com* and *http://ssl.bing.com/ listing*. It should also feature on search engine maps.

You can list for free in:

    www.dmoz.org

    www.freeindex.co.uk

    www.bttradespace.co.uk

    www.business-directory-uk.co.uk

    www.mylocalservice.co.uk

    www.uksmallbusinessdirectory.co.uk

    www.scoot.co.uk

    www.thebestof.co.uk

    www.businessmganet.co.uk

    www.toplocalservices.co.uk

    http://www.greenkey.co.uk

    http://www.webdetector.co.uk

    www.thefreewebsitedirectory.co.uk

    www.ukbusinesslisting.co.uk

    http://www.uklinkdirectory.co.uk

    www.the-free-directory.co.uk

    http://www.the-web-directory.co.uk

There are thousands of other web directories for the UK and millions worldwide. Most offer free listings; some may charge, or charge for a bigger display/advertising on the site and giving a link to your site. It is probably not worth paying for inclusion, although some photographers take advantage of free 30 day trails, to see if they get any response.

It is debateable whether or not to pay for advertising on the web, such as using Google AdSense pay per click, so your page is featured in the right hand column when the words you have chosen are searched for on Google. However, many do—studios and wedding photographers in particular.

There are also social bookmarks links you can put on your site, such as Delicious, Digg, Reddit and StumbleUpon, which can help increase your reach and impact of SEO words.

RSS Feeds

RSS (Really Simple Syndication) feed is an automated way of sending updates to your customers. If a visitor to your website subscribes to your RSS feed, they will automatically receive notifications whenever that particular content is updated. This feed is read using RSS reader software. The software can be web-based or installed directly onto a PC or other hardware device, e.g. a smart phone.

RSS feeds let your customers stay up-to-date with relevant content without needing to revisit the website. RSS feeds work best if your content changes regularly, for instance, you add new work every day/week, or blog regularly. For more information, see *www.businesslink.gov.uk*

Video sharing

It can be worth making a short video and uploading it to the internet. The main video sharing sires include: YouTube, Metacafe, Daily Motion, Vimeo, Break, Blip.tv, Google Video, Yahoo! Video, VidiLife, Stickam, Rewer and Video Egg. Many photographers use videos on their own sites as well as on video sharing sites to promote their work and books. Some just talk to camera, others demonstrate a photography technique or record a shoot, showing how they work. Others film short testimonials from happy clients, showing the work as well. Some combine music with a short slide show of appropriate images. You should ensure there are no copyright issues when using the music recordings of others.

Blogs

A blog is a good way to get your name and work known and to increase traffic to your website. Posting regular articles on topics such as street fashion, design, architecture, etc., will all help push people to your site when they use search engines. It may be tempting to blog about photography but on the whole, little work comes from other photographers.

The more frequently you post on your blog, the better. You can also invite comments. You could also start a photoblog, posting your photos. The most successful are usually thematic, concentrating on one chosen field of photography. Make sure you still have captions with SEO words.

Some photographers use blogs as marketing tools that lead to greater things. Scott Schuman, (*www.thesatorialist.com*), for example, has a photoblog on street fashion. It has led not only to more work as a fashion and street fashion photographer, but also to work as a columnist and fashion advisor. Some of the best photoblogs can be found on LIFE.com annual photoblog awards. See also *www.coolphotoblogs.com* and *www.photoblogs.org*.

Some photographers have moved from blogs to Facebook and Twitter. It is inadvisably to have just a blog or Facebook page and no website. Picture editors do not want to see the photos you took last week when on holiday.

Blogs and photoblogs can also attract advertising, especially if they are niche based, or you become an important visual commentator on fashion or cars, for example. As this is a public space, like your website, photographs should be of very high quality.

You can start a free blog with services such as Google Blogspot or Wordpress. Both are very easy to use and offer free design templates. You can add content of words and photos at any time. If not using your own domain name, (which invariably means a fee) your blog will have the company's name in the address: (http://your name.theirname.com). You can have a blog integrated as part of your website or put a link on your blog to your website.

Using Social Media

While social media and blogs can be valuable marketing tools, they are also fraught with dangers. Several magazines, for example, *Business Week*, now have a clause in their contract stating that photographers and journalists (staff or freelance) cannot post assignment details, or photographs from them, on Facebook, Twitter, blogs or any other social media until the photos and story have been published. This does make sense as competitors may scoop an idea.

It may seem innocent enough to you to Tweet you are on the M4 to Bristol to photograph X but you may alert a rival to a potential story. Your Facebook posting that you have just photographed a fabulous new ebook reader for such and such a company may scupper a big launch announcement. Confidentiality is vitally important. Nor should you ever criticise or insult anyone, in any media, including letter or email. You could be sued for defamation of character.

Some photographers use social sites and photo sharing sites such as Facebook, Flickr or Photobucket as well as a website. When people search for images, yours stand a better chance of being seen if you have your pictures in several places. Just be aware of terms and conditions of posting pictures on any social media, and whether you are inadvertently giving away any rights or in danger of work being 'stolen'.

LinkedIn

As discussed in networking, this is a good place to join industry groups of other professionals, not just photographers.

Facebook

You can also use Facebook to drum up business, get your name known, create a following, post testimonials, join groups of people in different industries who may want a photographer and connect to other photographers.

Google+

Google's rival to Facebook is already gaining ground and it is worth joining as another form of marketing.

Twitter

It can be worthwhile using Twitter to create a following, or to 'follow' another photographer. Some picture editors, photography directors and art directors also use Twitter, which can give you a connection, however tenuous, if you become a follower, when you want to present your portfolio.

There are, of course, other social networks like *www.xing.com*, another networking site for professionals, but Facebook, Google+ and Twitter dominate at the moment.

> *http://wallblog.co.uk* has useful articles on using social media.

> The American Society of Media Photographers, *www.asmp.org*, has an excellent article on social media and copyright.

If you want to read some good articles about web design, SEO words, getting more traffic, affiliate marketing etc., look at the site of the excellent web design company, *www.lineofsite.co.uk*. The site also gives prices for designing sites of a range of pages, so is a good guideline as to what you should be paying for a bespoke, high quality web site design service.

Business Stationery

A business card is essential and larger business cards (postcard/A5) suit the photographer better, although some have small business cards as well. If your A5 card has a fabulous picture and your name underneath, it may well be pinned to a board. It acts as a constant reminder of your existence. Most successful photographers constantly update their cards with new images.

Hundreds of local printers and online businesses offer card printing–some better quality than others. You need good quality card (some special offers of free or dirt cheap cards are on very thin card). Check for special offers and student discounts. **See Chapter Nine for a list of reputable card printers.**

Most online print services allow you to upload a photograph or two and your own pdf artwork for words, with a choice of fonts and sizes for wording. Most will also print large cards, postcards, letterheads, complement slips and labels.

Good print companies offer a wide range of logo design templates which can then be used to establish your 'brand', your identity. However, these will also be available to others and often the logo design quality is not brilliant. You could use a designer for something unique. Your logo should be used on your website, headed paper, complement slips, invoices and labels. A strong logo aids the visual memory (stronger than the verbal memory). If you do decide to use a designer, you might post your project on *www.peopleperhour. co.uk, www.elance.com* or *www.freelancer.co.uk* and ask for bids.

On business cards, you need to include your name and the word Photographer (you would be amazed at how many photographers forget this). If you want to be known as a specialist, you might put, for example, 'Performance and events photographer', or 'portraits and weddings photographer'. Some photographers have several business cards, to use according to circumstance.

You should also put your home town and country. Full addresses are not strictly necessary and for security reason may be unwise, given it indicates your home is full of expensive camera gear. Your card must include a phone number, your email and website address.

If you have invoices printed and are VAT registered, you must include the VAT number. You do not need to have your VAT number printed on letterheads—if you use a letterhead as an invoice, simply type on the VAT number, the tax point and date when you write the invoice. You can reclaim the VAT on the costs of printing. You can also offset stationery printing and web design costs against your tax.

Postal Mailshots

A new photocard is a good excuse for a new mailshot to existing and potential clients. Some photographers will also produce a variety of postcards and greeting cards, to send at Christmas, as thank you cards, etc.

Keeping in Touch

It is important that you can pick up your emails wherever you are, so a web-based email account is more useful than, for example, Outlook Express, although you can get emails re-rerouted to a web-based service. Also, if your computer dies, you will not lose all your emails if you use a web-based service.

A mobile phone is, of course, essential and most mobiles also allow you to pick up your email. It will have voice mail too. Just beware the costs if you are abroad.

It is advisable to make a contact database and keep copies on DropBox, SugarSync, Subversion, CloudApp or similar off site storage, so it is securely held offsite.

Public Relations

It is very satisfying to see your work in print, perhaps winning a photography magazine competition which then features in a magazine or exhibition. You may also win a good prize. Great. But how much work is that going to get you? How is it going to get your name known outside the world of photographers, who are not the ones commissioning or buying? You need greater reach.

If you do win a competition or bursary or have an exhibition coming up, you should shout about it. The competition organisers may well arrange their own public relations and press releases and it is worth checking if they will. If they don't intend to do any PR, send your own press releases.

A press release, with a photo attached can be sent to all sorts of media outlets, from national and local press, trade press, websites to local TV and radio. Target your release. Pick the right magazines (not just photographic ones) and newspapers, and the right sections within those publications. *www.mediauk.com* gives a good list of UK media. If you are soon to have an exhibition, ensure it goes to all the listings magazines and listing sections within the national and local press, as well as to 'what's on' websites and local forums.

The easiest way to send your press release is to use a PR wire company for distribution. It means they do the hard work of distributing it to all the relevant press contacts—you don't need to search every newspaper and magazine, for example, to find the name of the editor of the news or arts sections. A good PR distribution service should also tell you if it has been used, and where and when. However, while a few of PR wire services offer a basic free service, most do make a charge. Also, as most press releases are distributed via email, yours may be just another in an overcrowded in-box. There is something to be said for snail mail. Everyone opens their post.

In order to stand any chance of being used, a press release must cover something new, (whether it is the subject of the shot, or about you) and not just 'here I am, available for work'.

Press releases need attention grabbing headlines: 'Joe Bloggs is travelling to South America' is not a headline. 'Manchester Photographer Joe Bloggs Wins XX Travel Bursary' is better. Try and keep press releases to one page, or two at the most and under 500 words. Use headed paper at least for page one. Double space copy. If sending by post, staple second page to the first and include a print (6x9 is fine), with details of how to get more high resolution pictures. If you send by email, the same catchy headline should go in the subject line. If sending outside the UK, under the headline in the release, put the town and country that says where the press release originated. Caption and credit photographs—a sticky label on the back if posting, or at the end of the copy or in metadata if emailing. Snail mail is invariably better and it won't get consigned to the spam box.

Your press release should look like this:

PRESS RELEASE

Issued: (date)

For Immediate Release OR Embargoed Until: (date)

TITLE (keep it brief and attention-grabbing)

The first sentence should be a summary of the story. Get your key points across to catch the journalist's attention. Like good articles, always answer the important questions: who, what, where, when, why & how. Write as if you are speaking to the publication's readers—and always write in third person.

Expand on the details in the second paragraph. Remember the journalist will want to know what is unique or new about your story and why it will appeal to their readers. Then back up your claims with facts and statistics in the following paragraphs.

Illustrate your story with quotes; *"A quote, written in italics, from you and/or a key person, helps bring a story to life"*. Finish with details such as dates, times, how to order or contact you– this only needs to be brief, and should be the details you'd like to see in print. Fuller details can go in 'notes to editors', below.

Add the word **Ends** before notes to editors.
Then add

Notes to editors

1. Tell the editor who to contact for more information. Include your mobile and landline numbers and email. State that 'your name' is available for interview.

2. Include short background information on you (or your company), your training, exhibitions, where work has been used or exhibited, for example: 'Joe Bloggs is a Manchester based travel photographer who trained at X and won the Z competition. His work has been exhibited at... His work has appeared in (name a few main publications/ads etc)

3. Add 'For more examples of Joe Bloggs' work, please see (give your website address).

4. Attach one or two prints or email one/two pictures. Put low resolution photos in the body of the email, with high resolution photos as an attachment, If emailing photos, state what form they are in (ie, RGB, Jpeg, Tiff etc). State that these photographs are free to use solely if used with information in this press release and must be credited to (your name as you want it credited). Give brief captions of around 50–100 words.

Evaluating Press Coverage

There is no guarantee that any press release will be used and editors will not appreciate pestering phone calls asking if they are using it. Unless you employ an expensive press cuttings agency, or pay for it via a PR wire service, you will not necessarily know where and when your press release/ photo (supplied for free usage with press releases) has been used. Nor is the press release likely to be used in full—the sub editors will probably rewrite it to fit their house style and space. It may end up as a two line caption.

Unless someone commissions you on the strength of what they have seen and read and tells you so, you are not going to know how effective PR is. That doesn't mean you shouldn't do any PR. Think of it as a long time marketing strategy, with a drip-drip effect. Raising your profile in the press may not bring returns today or tomorrow but may well have a longer term effect on the memory of a commissioning editor or image buyer.

Email Marketing

Emails and mailshots can be sent to commissioning editors and industry contacts. You can even send it to family and friends and ask them to forward it to their email address book, as part of a viral marketing campaign. Email marketing is an easy and cheap way to make contact, keep people informed and keep you in their consciousness. Emails can inform people of special offers, exhibitions, awards etc. Some photographers use Facebook and/or Twitter instead of, or as well as, email marketing. Emails sent once a month are probably enough, so long as you have something to say. Don't expect a huge response to email marketing or mailshots. 1% is a good, 5% is very good.

If you are sending regular marketing emails or newsletters, you do need to be aware of the Data Protection Act—you must give people the option of opting out of receiving emails and unsubscribing to newsletters.

Spam filters are used by most internet service providers, preventing some emails from getting through, or being automatically consigned to email bins. Spam filters tend to target particular words, so avoid using words like Free, Save, Discount, £££ in the subject line and content of the email.

If an email contains too much text and graphics, it can put people off reading it. Keep it simple and clear in design. Featuring your website link in bold blue text is usually more effective than using a banner or button. Personalised emails–addressing people by name–are always better received than emails starting 'Hello' or 'Dear Sir/Madam'.

Online research analysts say that Tuesday and Wednesday are the best days to send emails. Thursdays are not a good idea for weekly publications as it is often press day. Before 3pm is best for all publications. Some analysts say that emails sent between 2-3pm (GMT) get most response. Always add your signature (name, address or partial address, phone number and a link to your website).

Creating an Email Newsletter

An email newsletter (so long as it is interesting) can be a very good way of reaching audiences. A newsletter to people you don't know, unless very long, is probably best kept as an email, as not everyone will open attachments. Keep the newsletter design consistent from issue to issue by creating a template. Use a catchy headline in the subject heading, for example: 'Your Name/newsletter no 1: How photography put £20k on the sale of this house.'

Chapter Six

Portfolios

*C*ommissioning decisions are as much about you and your personality as it is about your work. It goes without saying that your work is fabulous and you are presentable. While the client may have looked at your work on your website, you will still need a physical portfolio. This is true whether or not you have an agent representing you.

Your portfolio should always be tailored to meet the requirements of the client you are seeing. There is little point in having glorious landscapes to show to the picture editor of a fashion magazine.

Design companies and advertising agencies may want a unique style, so you could show personal work. If you have done work for a rival agency, a print of the photograph is usually better than a tear sheet (agencies are sometimes a bit dismissive of the work of rivals), with the final printed tear sheet at the back of the book.

However, if you are going directly to a client, (which is rare with large clients) rather than through a design or ad agency, a tear sheet showing your work in another company's ad, for example, can instil confidence—if X trusted you and used your work, they can too.

You could take your laptop, but don't just say 'it's all on my website'. Neither should you put your work on a disc or USB stick as few clients will let you use their computers. A lot of photographers now use iPads to show their work, which seems to go down well.

If you are not using an iPad, you need a traditional portfolio (sometimes called your 'book'). This is often a portfolio with plastic sleeves into which you slide your prints. Make sure plastic sleeves are clear, not too thick, don't create reflections or get scratched easily. Most portfolios are ring-bound, so you can easily change and add photographs, change the order so it is tailored the client you are seeing.

Some photographers show their work mounted on boards, which they keep loose in their portfolio or a presentation box, allowing them to easily change their selection of boards and tailor the ones they show to each client. Many feel their work looks better without a plastic cover/sleeve.

Some photographers produce printed photo books using print on demand (see **Publishing**). These days, they are not that expensive to produce but take care over paper, print and finish quality. However, once bound, photo books are inflexible and you may well need a portfolio as well.

Editing Your Photographs for Portfolios

It is tempting to put in a bit of everything, regardless of whether it is relevant to the client. 'If in doubt, leave it out' is a wise adage, as is 'less is more'. Leave out any photographs that are average, as they diminish the impact of good shots. Ideally, 20–30 good shots are enough. Try to create links between images, so the portfolio has some cohension.

If you are starting out, set your own project briefs and keep photographing, adding to your portfolio or replacing less good shots. Don't start your portfolio with a great shot followed by others in diminishing quality.

It really is worth spending some money to get high quality prints. A4 is good and A3 is more than big enough, though you might add some pace to your portfolio by having some bigger than others. An A3 portfolio will be fine, though many photographers have A2. Remember, you have to carry it. Be careful getting prints made at a size that does not have the same size ratio as your camera: the machines will crop the sides off. Ask for the whole image to be printed but on say A3 or A2 paper and trim it down with a scalpel.

Attached your business card to the inside cover of the portfolio in case you have to leave it with the client. Have copies of your A5 photo card to leave. You might also put in a short cv, with contact details, where you can mention your awards, competitions wins, experience etc. Remember, this is business, so no academic treatise on the meaning of your photography.

Mounting Your Work

Scalpels, blades, metal rulers and cutting boards can be bought in most art shops. If you can't afford a cutting board, always cut with a metal ruler on flat (not corrugated) cardboard. A set square is a good idea, to ensure lines are straight. Cutting card or photos along the ruler several times with only a little pressure is better than trying to press down hard and cut in one go.

If you are mounting prints on card, lay the photo on and see approximately where it looks best. Measure to ensure side margins are equal. Very lightly mark the corners with a sharp, soft pencil. Some professional picture framers like to leave a little more margin at the bottom as it visually makes the photograph 'float'.

Spray mount is best for photographs (available in art shops). You need to put down newspaper, onto which you put your photograph. Make sure the room is well ventilated or spray outside. It cannot be stressed enough that this is glue and not good to breathe in. Spray lightly and quickly over the whole back of the photo in one direction and then in the other. Count to 20 before you carefully place the photo on the card with corner meeting your pencil marks. You can use the metal ruler to align down one edge if you want and butt your photograph edge against it. Smooth down with a tissue.

If you get marks/fingerprints on your prints that don't come off when gently wiped with a tissue, try wiping with a little lighter fuel on a clean cloth.

You can also buy rolls of small double sided sticky tape tabs, which can be put in each corner on the back of your photos. Use an extra couple along the middle edges, if the print is large. It is not ideal, but it means you can detach your photographs if necessary.

Portfolio Reviews.

Many photo galleries, stock agencies, photographic courses/workshops and individuals run portfolio reviews. Magnum, the consortium of the world's top photojournalists, runs workshops in the UK on Professional Practice which often includes portfolio reviews–see *www.magnumphoto.com*. A charity called Ideas Tap, *www.ideastap.com*, offers bursaries to allow younger photographers to attend these events.

Search for any photo festivals that are happening near you and whether there are any workshops and portfolio reviews on offer—they are often free or charge much less than those who offer portfolio reviews as a business. Some university photography courses will offer free portfolio reviews at open days.

Chapter Seven

From the Horse's Mouth

Standards

It is assumed, even if you are starting out, that you are a good photographer. However, there is good and very good and excellent. Be honest with yourself, get your work critiqued and don't pitch above your present level. Think too about your other skills, of organisation, time-keeper, reliability, working under pressure and ability to follow a brief, handle crises and criticism.

There is no point arranging to see the picture editor at National Geographic until you are sure your work is as good as that of their other photographers. There is no point seeing the art director of Vogue when the fashion photos in your portfolio are more suited to a regular brand catalogue. Go and see the picture editors and art directors too soon, with lesser quality work than they expect, and it is possible they will never see you again. Wait. Learn, practice, improve and when you feel on a par with the best in that field, then make contact.

Follow these tips from top art directors and picture editors on approaching and working for them. These quotes are taken from many conversations the author has held during her years as picture editor of Time-Life and from interviews as a regular writer for *Hot Shoe* magazine. There is also advice especially for readers of this book from current top picture editors.

Do

◆ Find out my name, and spell it correctly. For magazines, we are listed on every masthead so it's not difficult. Or ring the reception and ask.

◆ Email me (addressing me by name) with a little about yourself, where you are based and what you have done, and a link to your website. Leave it for a few weeks before calling me to discuss you work. Put your phone number on your email.

◆ Get an under-designed website (not just a Facebook page please), with no flash, no music, easy to read text and clear images. It should be very easy to navigate, with no registration (I never register), no 'click here to enter my site'. Use image sizes that don't take an age to download. Keep it simple—I am a busy person.

◆ Be a collaborator, work with me, not for me.

◆ If we meet, have something to say about your pictures. Not that you are influenced by Jeff Wall and feel it is a post-modernist statement on whatever .... 'I took this in Sheffield for X and the light was amazing.' Or 'It's not the shot X company chose for their campaign but I really like the atmosphere...' something like that will do.

◆ If I invite you in to show your portfolio, have a photo card attached to a short cv you can leave with me. I may love your work but have to convince the editor or client. A small self-portrait on one side of your card, with a great image or two on the other (at least an A5, not a small business card which will get lost), will help me remember you. I see hundreds of photographers—make it easy for me to remember you.

◆ In your portfolio, put what is relevant–or might be–to me and the photos you are passionate about.

◆ Some photographers have work that is not very good but which they think is great. In fact, it is often very mediocre or in the style of the moment or the style of an established really good photographer. I want something new, not a Nick Knight. If I wanted that style, I'd ask him.

- Study at least 12 issues of my magazine..if you can see your work in it, great, call me.

- By all means put in some of your work that you do for yourself, but after work you have done for others.

- Put in less, not more in your portfolio. I can always tell when a portfolio has photos just there to fill it up.

- Show me previously commissioned work,–it's a telling way of seeing how you've approached and executed a brief.

- I get hundreds of emails and calls from photographers and agents every week. I want someone who can show the world in a new and different light, provoke, engage, make us think harder.

- I mainly look at websites first and if I am interested, then invite the photographer in with his or her portfolio. Send me a link to a website of work with a brief explanation of what you've been shooting, what your aim was, how you went about it etc.

- I don't want to see tear sheets of work in other magazines.

- Be reliable, professional and pleasant to work with—I hate prima donnas or know-it-alls.

- The photographers I commission are ambassadors for this magazine. As such, they must be professional, pleasant and treat all others well, whether in the office or outside, or it reflects badly on us and on you.

- I hate over-demanding and difficult people in any field. The photographers who get the best out of commissions are always very polite, considerate and never shout.

- I can spot talent in a portfolio even if the work is very different from what I might have in mind.

- If I commission you, accept that I know what I want and follow my brief.

- I will commission photographers primarily on the quality of their work, but I need to like them, want to work with them and know we are on the same wavelength.

◆ I often get emails of just one line, 'here is a link to my website'. I always delete them. They show no understanding about forging a relationship with a photo editor.

◆ Turn your phone off when we meet.

◆ Study my magazine and be aware of the individual editorial departments, then you can say 'I have a great set of images for an idea for the food and drink section or an epic journey for the travel section.'

◆ If you have shot a whole story and want to sell it, put in captions, not text. We rarely use a photographer to write the story. Great photos that don't tell a story are no use to us.

◆ If you have an idea for a story, write a couple of paragraphs explaining it. Don't be surprised if your 'unique' story idea is turned down. We come up with hundreds of story ideas every week and may have already run it or dismissed it.

◆ Be determined, not pushy. Have confidence in the work you are showing.

◆ If you are commissioned and the art director or picture editor attends the shoot, discuss the approach and follow his/her advice.

◆ With editorial photographs I'm looking for the truth and the photographer's view in revealing something. You're looking through the photographer's eye and seeing how he translates his insight into an image. It's a rare skill.

◆ I will commission young/starting out photographers but only so long as I think they will deliver. Sometimes, however, you need a tried and tested safe pair of hands.

◆ If I commission you, always keep in mind the magazine's vision and style. Discuss your concepts with me before you shoot.

◆ If photographing celebrities in a studio or their home, time will be very limited. Make sure you know your technical stuff inside out. Using your camera should be second nature.

◆ We have specific requirements for each job. Understand and meet them.

- We need photographers who will solve problems, not ring us in a panic.

- For editorial work, I want to see portfolios of photographs that are emotive or amazingly powerful or just beautifully informative.

- Make sure the end results are on message, meet the brief, and are right for our magazine.

- On a shoot, know how to put people at ease. Talk to them, make them laugh, offer them coffee, get them to relax. Tension shows.

- Even though I am commissioning editorial, I like to see ads and other shoots, to see your approach and styles.

- For editorial, and indeed most photographs, observe, use your mind and guts through the lens.

- Take pictures honestly, not contrived. Keep them simple—a good simple image says more than one where people have to work out what the hell is going on.

- For a photo essay or any photograph for that matter, the image should add information to the story or even be the story.

- Show me something I haven't seen before.

- Take the advice you are given by picture editors and art directors.

- I expect the photographer to answer the brief but still add their creativity and personality. I want to work with photographers who give that little bit extra.

- I want to see some originality.

- Meet the deadlines.

- Keep banging on doors.

Don't

- Don't mock up ad or editorial pages from my magazine with your photographs in it—just show me the photographs.

- Don't tell me how good you are. Many photographers have a very high opinion of their work, and tell me how brilliant it is. I can judge that for myself.

- Don't copy the style of established photographers. Show your own spirit. I see so much work that is derivative. Find your own voice.

- Don't bring in work that is totally inappropriate for my magazine. I edit a high end fashion magazine, so I don't want to see photos of down and outs under the arches.

- Don't chew gum while talking to me.

- Don't offer to buy me lunch/drink. I am not a date.

- If you can't see your pictures on my page, wait until you can. Come in too soon and it's doubtful we'd ever see you again.

- Don't be afraid to contact me. Even if you are fresh out of college, I am happy to offer advice if I have time.

- Don't say 'I can shoot anything'. I prefer photographers who are passionate about what they like to shoot and who have definite preferences of how they like to shoot.

- Don't go on about how, on X shoot, you flew to the Seychelles with ten lovely models, when we are in a studio in Hackney photographing pots of jam.

- Don't email huge attachments—we never open attachments unless we know who they are from.

- Don't try and be good at everything.

- Don't have all your eggs in one basket. The picture editor retires, the art director goes to New York—people do move on and it may leave you with no contacts. The new people may want to use their own choice of photographer.

- Don't cram your portfolio full of too many incoherent images; edit it down to a 'sound bite' of your strongest work. It's always appealing to see some structure in a photographer's portfolio.

- You'd be amazed at how many inappropriate portfolios I see. It should be relevant and changed and edited for every portfolio presentation.

- Don't think you are the bee's knees. Maybe you do have a degree, even a first, maybe you did win some award, but you are only as good as your last picture. Actually, you are only as good as your next one.

- Don't talk money/budgets and ask me what fees I pay when I haven't so much as commissioned you or said I'd buy a picture.

- Don't demand to be flown first class.

- Don't call me on press day.

- Don't make excuses. Sometimes shots are hard to get, the weather is ghastly, the locals aggressive. I know it can be very demanding to fulfil the brief but don't ring me up to moan. Work out a way to get what I want (rather than what you want).

- I run an architectural firm. I won't commission anyone with anything other than architectural pictures in their book.

- Photographers are now expected to do their own retouching, so learning Adobe Photoshop or similar is essential.

- Photographers, especially news and sports photographers, are now expected to shoot video too. The Red One camera, for example, allows you to shoot HD video that can also be used immediately to produce high-resolution stills. Cheaper models are coming along all the time. Learn how to use them.

- We look for images that make you stop and look again. It is not usually one terrific shot but the whole portfolio that stands out.

- Don't pester me. If you are in with a chance, we'll be in touch.

- Don't forget our lead times. Monthly magazines work months ahead. Don't come in to sell me a Christmas story in November. I need it to see it in August.

- Don't overuse Photoshop but know how to use it.

- Don't use loads of film, even if film is your thing, without considering our budget. Digital is cheaper.

- Don't ignore what someone else says at a meeting. They may only be an editorial assistant/junior designer at present but we work as a team and one day, they may be editor.

- For photojournalism, be honest. Don't set things up or manipulate images to suit your story. Of course photographers edit by their eye but show the world and society as honestly as possible.

- If it's a portrait, I want the photographer to bring out the personality—don't show me a photo that doesn't show empathy with the subject,

- Budgets are constantly shrinking—ours have been cut by 50%. We are still expected to commission in the same way, producing the same standard and creativity, but for a lot less money. If I say the rate is X, it really is."

Advice Just For You

'How to approach me... Generally we don't encourage unsolicited portfolios but the fact is that once in a blue moon a new photographer will wow us with their unique style. My best advice would be, look at the magazine and if you can seriously see your work on the pages then get in touch. Otherwise wait until you are ready. If we see it and aren't impressed, it's unlikely we'll see you again for a long time.

What to include in (and leave out of) a portfolio/website. Make sure what you are showing is specific to that publication. Study every issue from the last 12 months from cover to cover and only show us work that you can actually see appearing on the pages of GQ. Otherwise, don't bother.

The biggest mistake photographers make when working for us the first time is bothering us with small problems. We are commissioning over fifty shoots a month as well as the masses of picture research, caption writing, negotiating and writing we have to do. Once you are commissioned and the concept is agreed make it as easy as possible for us. Most importantly, deliver what was agreed. Failure is never an *option. We always need the image that we have commissioned. Excuses as to why it didn't work out are not acceptable.*

I use someone unknown if they come to us with something new, fresh or even just simply amazing. Do something high concept that looks like it could be in GQ then I am interested. I do not want to see things that anyone could do.'

—James Mullinger, Photographic Director, *GQ*
www.twitter.com/jamesmullinger

'This sounds obvious but a photographer needs an easy to use and comprehensive website. You'd be surprised by the number of photographers who do not update their website or send links to their blog. Nowadays I like to see a website first and then if I think the work would be suitable for us I like to see a book and meet the photographer in person. A photographer is representing our magazine when I commission them and as we shoot a lot of portraits of people in their environments I need to know that the subjects are going to feel comfortable and happy.

I prefer a website that not only contains published images and commissions but that also shows me where the photographer wants to be going with their work and what their real interest is. Quite often the best/most interesting image is not necessarily the one that was published for various reasons and it is of more use to me to see what the photographer thinks is a great shot.

Every photographer needs a card and it needs to have a few images on it that best show their work. A small business card is of no use to me. I see a lot of photographers and within a week a name on a business card means nothing. I keep the cards of photographers that would be great to use on my desk so you need to stand out from the rest and best show me what you do.

Don't completely tailor your portfolio to what you think I want to see or what you think our magazine is about. Once I have seen your website and asked to meet you then I have already seen something I like. We need to use photographers with different styles and are always looking for new people to give a new perspective. That said, there is no point contacting me if your work is totally irrelevant as it shows a lack

The Bigger Picture

of knowledge of the product. We see a lot of photographers and of course are going to choose to work with the people who really want to work for us and understand the magazine.

A small thing which I advise against is blanket emailing. Make sure you know the name of the Picture Editor/Art Buyer/Art Director or Bookings Editor. This is a basic common courtesy plus blanket emails give the impression that you are contacting anyone and everyone in the hope that someone might offer you a job. You need to target who you want to shoot for and be relevant to them.'

—Beverley Croucher, Picture Director, *Red Magazine*
BeverleyCroucher@redmagazine.co.uk

'Know your market so you can supply the best and most original material.'

—Rebecca Hawtrey, Art Editor/Deputy Editor, *The Field*

'By far the best way to approach me is to send a link to a website along with a brief intro. If the website is uncomplicated & easy to navigate & shows editorial layouts I'm even happier. The worst way to approach me is to call and hassle me to call you back. The second worst way to approach me is to send images that aren't relevant. I delete so many photographers emails whose homepage image is Studio Portraiture or Fashion. If you want a Travel commission, only show Travel.'

—Polly Teller, Picture Editor, *Sunday Times Travel Magazine*
0044 207 782 7381

'How to approach me: a telephone call to introduce yourself, followed up by an email with portfolio details.

What I look for: A portfolio website need be nothing but relevant and current. Fancy gadgets, annoying download times, html bulk emails will all send me directly to the delete or close window button.

A photographer is only as good as their last assignment.

Mistakes: Do your homework, make sure you know the subject and style of the magazine. Don't try selling me pictures of something that has absolutely no relevance at all to the magazine. Don't try calling on press day unless it's directly about pictures for that issue, again this comes back to doing the homework.

We are always looking for new and upcoming talent. Age is irrelevant, so is equipment used. All I want to see is pin sharp pictures, of the moment and engaging to look at; something to hook our readers and grab their attention. A photographer who shows initiative and perseverance will be successful if their pictures match their ambitions.

Qualifications mean nothing to me: good quality pictures, delivered on time, well captioned and high resolution are all I care about. I don't mind if your other job is working at a fast food joint or working in a bar. It's very hard to make photography pay enough to live on by pure editorial work alone, it's worth keeping an open mind and working with other subjects and exploring all avenues to get the income to live on."

—Jayne Toyne, Picture Editor, Horse & Hound

Chapter Eight

Photographers' Agents

A photographer's agent is someone who will represent you, present your portfolio to prospective clients, hopefully get you commissions, handle the contracts, negotiate fees and chase payments. Clients will invariably still want to meet you but an agent can help get your foot in the door. They are adept at networking, making contacts and have no qualms about ringing art directors and picture editors to arrange to show them portfolios or to talk about the exciting new photographer s/he has just taken on.

If you hate 'selling' yourself, networking, negotiating fees, chasing payments, then getting an agent might be a route to go. Don't expect the work to flood in just because you have any agent—most agents have quite a few photographers on their books but they may suggest you if a job is up your street or you may get booked if the picture editor/art director likes your portfolio.

But to be worthwhile for you—and the agent—you must be reliable. No agent wants to get you work that you then can't, or won't, do. Agents run businesses and need to earn their living too through their commission. They will want employable, commercial photographers, whatever their field. Nor do they want a photographer on their books who brushes up clients the wrong way. Few agents will take totally untried photographers—so it is worth getting a few commissions under your belt before you even think of approaching an agent.

You should consider the agent's reach—will they sell you overseas, just in the UK or even just in London? It can pay to have an agent who either travels a lot on your (and other photographers') behalf or has an office/affiliate agencies abroad. Some top photographers have different agents in different countries. If you think there is a market for commissions in the Far East, for example, and are based in the UK, you may want a second agent out there. Do not sign an exclusive representation contract that stops you exploiting that region.

Agents, of course, take their cut and the commission is often quite high. 30-40% is not uncommon, although it can be 50% in some circumstances. If the thought of giving away a large percentage is too much, you could do the leg work yourself.

In the USA (less so in the UK) some photographers employ a person to act as agent solely for them or pay each time a freelance agent takes their work to show to a buyer, either combining the payment with–or instead of–commission.

Never sign up with the first agent who accepts you as a client. The main UK agents are listed here and some specialise in fashion or advertising photographers or represent only the very top photographers. Do look at their websites to get a feel if they are right for you, at your level. The agents' books may already be full and they may not wish to take on more photographers, even if you are brilliant.

Some agencies are not listed here, such as the consortium Magnum, which is made up of members of the best in the world, mostly photojournalists, and joining is by invitation.

Take time to study who else is on the agents' books. Some agents only want one of each type of photographer, for example, one food photographer, one specialist in fashion, in their stable. Others may specialise and want photographers in the same fields.

From the websites you have looked at, draw up a short list of, say, six appropriate agents. Look for signs that you'll fit in and will complement (rather than duplicate) the work and style of their existing photographers. Even in the same field, such as fashion, they will want each photographer to have his/her own distinctive style. Your work and style needs to be relevant to their client database.

It can be a good idea to look for an agent who is at a similar stage in their career. If you are just starting out, an agent doing the same might be perfect. If you are already making a name for yourself, an established agent might be better. If you are already a famous photographer, you will probably already have a top agent.

Email, (by name, not Dear Sir or Madam), express interest in being represented by them and put a link to your website address, plus give contact details—your mobile number especially. Make sure your website is perfect, works simply and effectively and shouts 'great photographer, snap me up or someone else will'. If they are interested, they should contact you.

If you haven't heard after about 8-10 days, email or phone again. Be polite and professional and ask if they have had time to look at your website and if they would be interested in seeing your portfolio (they will still want to see one, as often it is that they will be hauling in front of clients on your behalf). Some agents will accepting seeing (and even presenting) work on an iPad.

Certainly talk about your successes but don't come across as a prima donna. Explain why you are a good choice for them and what you can bring to the party. Agents are, like everyone in business, thinking, 'what's in this for me?' Remember that first impressions count: be presentable, charming without being smarmy, smile, thank them for seeing you. Get it wrong and you won't be asked back.

Getting an agent is a big step and should develop into a long-lasting business relationship. You must like each other and have the same business objectives. They should promote you, present your portfolio to buyers and be in regular contact with you, even if there is no work available. Ask about their clients, how long they have worked with them, who it is that presents portfolios to clients and how often they see art buyers. If your first meeting with the agent doesn't go too well, don't despair. Keep trying other agents.

Don't sign up until you have seen all your shortlist—just say, 'I'll give you time to think about it. Please do email if you have any further questions.' If you don't hear back, and you really liked the agent (very important) and felt they liked you and your work, email again asking if they have come to a decision. Don't be surprised if a reply takes a week or two—agents are (or should be) very busy people.

If you are taken onto an agent's books don't expect miracles overnight. View it as a long term business plan. Keep shooting even if you have no commissions, so you can send new pictures to update the agent's website. Your portfolio should also be kept up-to-date and fresh. A few months of an agent touting it round and lots of people thumbing through and it will soon need refreshing.

This list is not definitive but should be enough to get you started in the search for the perfect agent.

If you do find an agent and it doesn't work out and you leave, for whatever reason, keep those reasons to yourself. Like any business sector, the world of agents is a small one.

Photographers' agents UK

A Agency: www.aagency.co.uk

A and R Photographic Agency Ltd: www.aandrphotographic.co.uk

Abby Johnson: www.abbyjohnson.com

Alan Wickes: www.alanwickes.com

Andrea Walji: www.andreawalji.com

Annabelle Dalton: www.annabelledalton.com

Anthea Bowen: www.antheabowen.com

Agent Orange Photographers Agents: www.agentorange.co.uk

Agent Pandora: www.agentpandora.co.uk

Agent Sue Allatt: www.sueallatt.com

Agent Wendy Jackson: www.wendyjackson.co.uk

Alan Wickes: www.alanwickes.com

Alexandra von Ziechmann Photographers Agents: www.alexandravz.com

Alyson Jones: www.alyson-jones.com

Areia London: www.areia.com

Axiom Photographic Agency: www.axiomphotographic.com

Artist Representation Management: www.armanagement.org.uk

Balcony Jump Management Ltd www.balconyjump.co.uk

Big Photographic: www.bigactive.com

Blood & Co: www.bloodandco.com

Blunt Management Photographers Agents: www.bluntlondon.com

Burnham Niker Ltd Photographers Agents: www.burnham-niker.com

Catherine Collins: www.catherinecollins.co.uk

Carolyn Trayler Photographers Agents: www.trayler.co.uk

CLM Photographers Agents: www.clmuk.com

CSB Management Ltd: www.csbmanagement.com

Coy Communications: www.coy-com.com

CRE8 Photography: www.cre8photo.com

D+V Management: www.dandvmanagement.com

Darling Creatibe: www.darling-creative.com

David & Rose Lambert: www.davidlambert.com

David Edmunds Productions: www.lpa-folios.com/david_edmunds

David Esser Associates: www.esserassociates.com

East Photographic Ltd: www.eastphotographic.com

Edson Williams: www.edsonwilliams.com

Ellison Lee Ltd Photographers Agents: www.ellisonlee.com

ERA Management: www.eramanagement.com

Europe Unlimited: www.europeunlimited.com

Factory 311: www.factory311.com

Germaine Walker: www.germain.co.uk

Gill Turner Photographer's Agent: www.gillturner.com

Gina Phillips Represents: www.ginaphillips.co.uk

Horton-Stephens: www.horton-stephens.com

Icon Photo: www.iconphoto.com

Image: www.imageagents.co.uk

Jackie Gibbs: www.jackiegibbs.com

Jamie Stephen: www.jamiestephen.com

Jane Patrick: www.janepatrick.co.uk

Jo Clark: www.joclark.com

John Parkinson Agency: www.johnparkinsonagency.co.uk

Jo Talbot & Sue Young: www.talbotyoung.com

Joyce Morris: www.joycemorris.co.uk

Julian Cotton: www.juliancotton.co.uk

Katy Niker: www.burnham-niker.com

Lavinia Hughes: www.lharepresents.com

Lisa Pritchard Agency: www.lisapritchard.com

Looker London: www.lookerlondon.com

Lucid: www.lucidrep.com

Mark George: www.markgeorge.com

M & M Management: www.mmmanagement.com

M.A.P. Photographers Agents: www.mapltd.com

Metcalfe Lancaster: www.metcalfelancaster.com

Morgan Lockyer Ltd www.morganlockyer.com

Mutton Bones Ltd www.muttonbones.co.uk

Nick Michaelides Productions Ltd www.nmpphoto.co.uk

Noelle represents: www.noellerepresents.com

One Photographic: www.onephotographic.com

Patricia McMahon: www.patriciamacmahon.com

Peter Bailey: www.peterbailey.co.uk

Process: www.processphotography.com

Red Photographics Photographers Agents: www.red-photographic.com

Refresh Artist Management: www.refresh-agency.com

S Management: www.smanagement.co.uk

Santucci and Co: www.santucciandco.com

Sarah Kaye Representation: www.sarahkaye.com

Sarah Daw Photographers Agents: www.sarahdaw.com

Sarah Lane: www.sarahlanerepresents.com

Sharon Brandman Agency: www.sharonbrandman.com

Shoot Production Ltd: www.shootgroup.com

Soho Management: www.sohomanagement.co.uk

Siobhan Squire: www.siobhansquire.com

Stella Pye Photographers Agent: www.stellapye.com

Sue Allatt: www.sueallatt.com

Swerve: www.swerverepresents.com

Terri Manduca: www.terrimanduca.co.uk

Terrie Tanaka Management: www.terrietanaka.com

The Angela Woods Agency: www.angelawoods.com

The Katy Barker Agency Ltd: www.katybarker.com

The Miss Jones Agency: www.themissjonesagency.com

The Peter Bailey Company: www.peterbailey.co.uk

The Pure Agency: www.thepureagency.co.uk

Trayler & Traylor: www.trayleyandtraylor.com

Van Hauen Moore Photographers Agents: www.vanhauenmoore.com

Vue: www.vue-us.com

Wyatt-Clarke & Jones: www.wyattclarkejones.com

Z Photographic: www.zphotographic.com

Other agents may be found on in the Marketing and Creative Handbook, www.mch.co.uk, and Creative Handbook, www.chb.com and on www.photoagentslondon.co.uk, www.productionparadise.com, www.kays.co.uk, www.filefxagent.co.uk.

Chapter Nine

Prints, Products and Books

*T*here is a huge market in products using photographs. In shops, there are cards and calendars, mousemats and mugs, all using photographs. In markets, craft shows, local events, there invariable are a few photographers selling prints, cards, calendars, mugs, place mats, keyrings, coasters, t-shirts etc., all using their own work. Some even buy the rights to photos by others, often via microstock or direct from other photographers, which they then manufacture into products to sell.

Your local council will be able to advise on taking market stalls (which you may need to provide or rent). Local arts organisations and the arts department of your local council should be able to advise on forthcoming craft and art fairs. You could also try a pop-up shop, using an empty premises. Work can also be sold to shops, online shops, and directly from online 'shopping malls', like *www.etsy.com* or auction sites such as eBay.

Neil Williams, one of the UK's best landscape photographers, mounts and frames large prints of his work to sell. This he does on the pavement on Saturdays (for which he presumably got a licence from the council) in East Dulwich, South East London. His work is fabulous and while his prices are not low, offering prints for sale in an up-and-come area of mainly young professional is evidently worthwhile for him.

www.neilwilliams.co.uk

Another photographer has his photographs incorporated into glass beer mats which he sells as souvenirs. The photos are not the usual tourist shots but close-ups of items such as a lock, clock, or street sign featuring, for example, the word 'London'. They have the advantage that they are unusual, look very attractive and classy and are small enough to be the ideal souvenir for tourists. He takes a stall in a London market popular with tourists where he sells them at around £6–8.

If you want to try something similar, you can buy glass coasters into which you slide your photographs from £1.99 on Amazon, which may be a good way to test the market. Of course, you also have print costs and any costs for taking a market stall or table at a fair.

You could also try getting other products personalised with your work—not just coasters but key-rings, badges, magnets, placemats, photo-bags, wallets, cushions, T-shirts, aprons, mugs, jigsaws, chopping boards, keepsake boxes, sports items, money boxes. Many firms offer to personalise items with your own photographs but at a price. You may want to talk to them about trades prices.

The firms listed here are some of those that specialise in printing work onto canvas, acrylic or even aluminium, often used for wall art, place mats and coasters. Some are trade only, some trade and public. Photographers are advised to make it clear they are trade customers.

Acrylicize—www.acrylicize.com

Acrylic Pictures—www.acrylicpictures.com

Acrylic Image—www.acrylicimage.com

Artcrylic–www.artcrylic.co.uk

Artylicious Canvas Art—www.artylicious.co.uk

Bigphotoshop—www.bigphotoshop.co.uk

Eyecandy Art Group—www.eyecandyartgroup.com

Canvas101—www.canvas101.co.uk

CanvasRus—www.canvasrus.co.uk

Canvas Imagery—www.canvasimagery.co.uk

Eyes Wide Digital Ltd—www.eyeswidedigital.com

Fabio Art Ltd—www.fabioart.co.uk

Four Blank Walls—www.fourblankwalls.co.uk

Fruit Art—www.fruitart.co.uk

Image Shed—www.imageshed.co.uk

Photobloc—www.photobloc.com

Picture Crystals Ltd—http://picturecrystals.co.uk

Point101—www.point101.com

SCL Imaging Group—www.sclimaging.com

SolutionsDigital—www.solutions-digital.co.uk

Spafield Displays ltd—www.spafield.co.uk

The Digital Room—www.thedigitalroom.co.uk

Tocco Photos on Canvas & Acrylic—www.toccoinside.co.uk

Welcome Products—www.welcomeproducts.com

Willinspire Ltd—www.willinspire.com

Wriggly-tin—www.wriggly-tin.com

If you want to make something in greater numbers, there is the cost of production and invariably a large minimum order. The more you get made, the lower the unit cost but it does means laying out an often considerable sum. Manufacturing in the UK is more convenient but often the costs won't leave you able to add much for profit and still achieve a price that people will pay.

You could consider getting goods, using your photographs, manufactured abroad, and China is still a favourite. There will be a minimum order (perhaps 500-1000 units), there will also be import duty to pay, transport costs from the port to your home/storage unit and exchange rate fluctuation (most Chinese firms quote in US dollars). You may also need secondary suppliers to help with the trading process, such as freight forwarders or import agents to handle shipping and customs-related formalities and documentation.

However the unit cost of getting something produced in China (or India, Korea, Thailand etc.,) is likely to be much lower than in the UK, even taking these extra costs into account. Remember, the higher number of any product you order, the lower the unit cost of each item. It does mean finding some capital up front so be sure of your market first. It is always worth testing the market before you order large quantities of goods, even if you are, at first, selling at very low or no profit. If there is high demand, you can then consider placing higher orders.

If you have no idea of how to find a manufacturer in China, and other countries, contact UK Trade and Investment, *www.ukti.gov.uk*, a government body for advice on import and export. A trade association may also be able to help, as might the British Chamber of Commerce, *www.britchamb.org* and the appropriate British Embassy listed at the Foreign and Commonwealth Office, *www.fco.gov.uk*. Your bank's trade services department may also be able to help you source a reputable manufacturer and help with import obligations and finance.

Selling Postcards, Greeting Cards, Calendars, and Prints

Calendars and cards demand very high quality, high resolution photography and excellent printing. The least financially risky route is to contact a producer of cards and calendars and sell them rights to use your work.

The market is worth billions and increasingly, online services offer cards and calendars personalised with your own photo, art work and names. While most traditional card companies tend towards illustration, some do use photographs. They tend to specialise in areas or topics, and their websites will show if your photographs might fit with the style used by that company.

You can also find card and calendar and wall-art print publishers at The Spring Fair, held every February, (usually at the NEC, Birmingham) where hundreds of such companies take display stands to present their wares to retail buyers. The website *www.springfair.com* lists all exhibitors. It is by no means every company in the industry but is a good start. There are offshoots of the Spring Fair, most notably Top Drawer. Some of the main card companies are also listed below.

The Spring Fair is also a good way to find suppliers of coasters, place mats, fridge magnets and all manner of goods that could incorporate your photographs.

The calendar and card companies' websites may give guidance about if and when they are looking at submissions—as most such businesses run on a seasonal basis, there may be certain times of year they look for new material. They are likely to start considering their summer collection many, many months ahead, in time to show retailer buyers at the Spring Fair in February.

It is best to email or write with an enquiry first before submitting, and/or to email a short letter with a few low resolution pictures in the email (explaining they are low resolution). Very few companies will open attachments from people they do not know. Most will only be interested in a set—few will take one-off photos. They rarely consider photographs that have already been published or are with a stock library.

Greetings Card rights or Calendar rights allows you also to sell the photographs to any non-competitive field, although some companies may want exclusive rights. Never be tempted to sell the same photograph to a rival company.

If the company would like rights to use your photograph it is worth asking them to make an offer but it shouldn't be less than £75 per photograph. You might agree to offer a discount if they want a whole calendar of your work or buy the rights to hundreds of photos.

Cards and Calendar publishers:

The Greetings Card Association: www.greetingcardassociation.org.uk (for a list of members)

Chris Andrew Publications: www.cap-ox.co.uk

Thomas Benacci: www.thomasbenacci.co.uk

GB Eye Ltd: www.gbeye.com

Hallmark Cards plc: www.hallmark.co.uk

Otter House Ltd/Images Editions: www.otterhouse.co.uk and www. images-editions.co.uk

Indigo Art Ltd: www.indigoart.co.uk

Infocado: www.infocado.co.uk

Judges Postcards Ltd: www.judges.co.uk

Kardorama Ltd: www.kardorama.co.uk

Photo Dimension: www.photodimension.co.uk

Pineapple Park Ltd: www.pineapplepark.co.uk

Portfolio Collection Ltd: www.portfoliocards.co.uk

Nigel Quiney Publications: www.nigelquiney.com

Riverside Cards: www.riversidecards.com

Rose of Colchester Ltd: www.rosecalenders.co.uk

J Salmon Ltd: www.jsalmon.co.uk

Santoro Graphics: www.santorographics.com

WPL: www.wpl.eu

You need to find the name of the art or photography buyer. Some sites give contact details or phone and ask. Some also give submission requirements on their sites, which should be carefully followed—an incorrect submission is likely to be binned without response.

Include in the email, and as an attachment, about six samples appropriate to them. If sending by post, six 6 x 9 inch prints will suffice, with a caption on the back and details of what dpi you can supply. Include a little of your experience in your field.

Study their range and what they have used in the past. Photographic cards printed with amusing captions are also popular: if you have the right shots and you can write a good tag line, you may be able to sell rights.

Do not pester the buyer. Wait for a response. You may not get one for weeks, if at all. After, say, three weeks of silence, email or phone and ask, politely, if they received your submission and if they are interested. If they ask for additional photographs to review, send them as soon as possible by whatever means they stipulate.

You could, of course, find a good litho printer and produce your own but to make enough margin to compete with the big boys, you need a high print run in order to lower the unit cost. You then have to sell them. If not selling direct to the public (at craft markets etc.,) you have to sell them to a wholesaler, who in turn sells them to a retailer. Or you can sell them direct to retailers. Photographers do make businesses out of their work, as can be seen by the number of photographers at various trade fairs, but they are likely to spend more time on selling and paperwork than taking photographs.

The following are some of the UK print companies who supply quality cards:

www.abacusprinters.co.uk

www.colourcards.co.uk

www.giraffecards.com

www.goodprint.co.uk

www.judges.co.uk

www.thepostcardcompany.com

www.thoughtfactory.co.uk

www.centralcardsprinting.com

www.uniquecards.org

www.loudmouth.co.uk

www.petrolcards.com

Approaching Retailers

You really need to have a range of cards and/or postcards/prints to show to buyers in shops and stores as they are usually not interested in one or two designs. You can, unless the retailer asks for exclusive supplies, sell them to many retailers although most will demand them on sale or return: if they don't sell, you have to take them all away and if you have been paid for the whole batch, refund them.

Some may want an exclusive deal: the store or shop group may well want its own name and logo on the back, designed to its own style, using its house typeface and printed to a certain size. If a retailer is interested, find out what they would want on the inside and reverse of the card, and how many they would order—and get an order in writing before you print.

If you do have cards printed, have a firm idea of pricing—most retailers want to at least double the price you charge them. They may demand a discount if they order a lot. If VAT registered, you have to add VAT to your selling price. Big retailers rarely deal with anyone who is not VAT registered.

Greeting cards and calendars will also need cellophane bags and an EAN bar code. You can get cello bags, as they are called, for cards of all sizes, from many packaging manufacturers, though there is often a minimum order number/spend. Smaller numbers are sold by suppliers on *www.etsy.com* and eBay.

It is not advisable to have 5000 cards printed of each of your ten best photos and hope to sell them—without an outlet, not only will the printing have cost you but your money is then tied up in unsold stock. Selling rights is easier and less risky, especially if the cards you had printed on the strength of an order are rejected because of a spelling mistake or poor printing quality.

Pricing Your Products

When pricing products you need to take not only production costs into account, but rent, rates, mileage, telephone, eating… Never be tempted just to base your pricing on production costs alone. Of course, your time is the big intangible in pricing, unless you set yourself a minimum: 'I won't do it unless I can make at least X per unit'. Work out all your expenses and add them to the production costs. Then divide by the number of cards (or keyrings) you have had made and it will give you a unit cost. Then add your profit, and you come to the price that you must charge a retailer (or the public, if selling direct). You can read more about costings on the Business Link website. It is always a bit of a gamble, as at this stage, you have no real idea of how many products you will sell unless you have an advance order.

The Psychology of Pricing

You will have noticed that most products are priced at say, £14.99 rather than £15. For some reason £14.99 sounds a whole lot cheaper than £15. Cards are also often priced at, for example, £3.49 rather than £3.50. Books have been written on the psychology of pricing but while it may seem daft to take the price down by 1p, it does work. If you have no idea how to price your products, look at the competition (unfortunately, there always is some). If their similar products are too low for you to compete, find a way to add value to yours. A presentation box, signing your work, a free second card, free ribbon, gift wrapping service, a discount voucher for 10% off future orders,—cost them into your price to make them appear more exclusive or perceived as better value. If selling online, free delivery also works.

Barcodes for Products Other Than Books

If you are hoping to sell to stores and shops or through most online shops you need an EAN barcode. If you are just selling for yourself on eBay and at local markets and fairs, you don't.

For a barcode, go to the official UK issuing body's site, *www.gs1uk.org*. You join GS1UK as a member, at a cost (2011 prices) of £102, plus VAT, and an annual subscription of £102, plus VAT. This gives you a licence to allow you to create up to 1000 bar code 13-digit EAN numbers for up to 1000 different product lines.

You need one bar code EAN number and the bar code artwork (GS1UK will send you a pack telling you how to do this when you join) for each print run of the same card, regardless of whether you print 10 or 10 million of each card. There are companies on the web that offer to resell you small quantities of bar code numbers (1 for £3, or 1 for £7.99 or 10 for £49.99, for example), without the need to join GS1UK, but be aware that they may not be unique numbers, the numbers may be registered to someone else and may not then work in stores or online stores.

Book Publishing
Traditional Publishers

Photographers do have books published by traditional publishers but it is not easy. Mostly, they are 'how to take better photographs' books. Most publishers will only go for big names and certainly getting published conventionally has never been more difficult if you are little known. Some photographers, but not many, have had books published, usually on a theme, such as The

Mountains of… or The Wildlife of… or as art/ retrospective photography books. More often, photographers team up with a writer to cover a specific subject. Traditional publishers increasingly only look at proposals that come from literary agents, although a photographer's agent may also approach them.

If accepted for publication by a traditional publisher, they will design your book, using your photos, at no cost to you. Traditional publishers take a risk on your book and print a certain number of copies, usually by litho. Their sales force will then try and get them into bookshops. Your book will also be available on Amazon and other online retailers. The publishers may pay you an earn-out advance, often very little these days. After your book has sold enough to cover that advance, you then get royalties. These can vary from around 7–15%. Royalties for paperbacks tend be lower than for hardbacks. Occasionally, they may pay more–or less.

They will also try and sell foreign rights so the book can be published in other countries, for which you are paid extra. They may need to produce a co-edition with a foreign publisher to make the finances work: a foreign publishing company agrees to take so many copies. The publisher arranges translation of text but the book design stays the same. The black printing plate is simply changed to the new foreign text which is printed instead.

You can find the names of publishers in *The Writers' and Artists' Yearbook*. Most good libraries should have a copy, although it is an inexpensive annual paperback. The book also gives the names of literary agents. There is also a list of publishers and agents worldwide on *www.publishersglobal.com*. Publishers and literary agents receive thousands of submissions and it may take months to even look at yours.

If approaching a publisher directly, make sure your proposal fits into their publishing programme. Browsing the bookshelves will give you the names of publishers who publish photographic books, or other books with photos in them (such as travel, wildlife, etc). You should then shortlist the publishers' names and look at their websites. Most give submission guidelines and the names of the commissioning editors.

You will also need to think about text. If you are not confident about your writing abilities, the publisher may suggest someone or you could search, or advertise for, a writer on one of the outsourcing sites for freelancers or on site like LinkedIn.

If employing a writer or even joining forces with one 'on spec', always have a written agreement about bylines, copyright, payment and deadlines. If the book is to be published solely under your name and text is inaccurate or even libellous, it will be your responsibility. Every book, whether conventionally published or self-published should have a legal disclaimer on the half-title page (the left hand page of information opposite the title page).

Self-Publishing

Some photographers will self-publish and get a lot of copies produced, printed litho, for the best quality. While a few manage to get sponsorship or a grant to help with the funding, it is still likely to be a very costly exercise. The unit cost of each may well be very high unless you have a huge print run, as the more you print, the lower the unit cost.

You have to send out review copies at your own expenses. You have to try and see the buyers of big bookshop chains (never easy). You also have to try and get them into other bookshops. Unless you are prepared to travel the length and breadth of the country, you can employ a distributor, for a cut, to sell for you. Bookshops will want at least 35–50 per cent of the retail price and will want books on a sale or return basis. Big chains and giants like Amazon will demand an even higher percent of the retail price. If you can't sell the books, you may be left with a full garage.

While we have some terrific printing companies in the UK, the Far East is often a cheaper place to print, even if you take shipping into account. The quality from some printers overseas can be astoundingly good. Imago Publishing Ltd (*www.imago.co.uk*) handles the production of illustrated books in the Far East for many big UK publishing companies. Beautiful books of photographs are also printed in Italy, where some printers are renowned for quality. Some printers in The Netherlands and Northern

Ireland also have a very good reputation. If you don't know where to start, a print buyer or book designer can help.

Generally, unless you can find a sponsor, self-publishing colour books printed by litho is really only suitable for those with deep pockets.

Photobooks

You can get a book produced as a photobook or through specialist print on demand photo (POD) book companies. POD colour books can cost under £20 a copy. However, if you want to sell it, the cost of producing it means that unless you can charge a very high price, there is not enough margin to make a profit. The higher the cost, the less likely people are to buy it. Remember too, that if you sell via third parties, such as Amazon, they will also want their cut.

Photographers are always concerned about quality. Albelli, Apple iPhoto, Cewe Books and Loxley Colour seem to come out as favourites on most photography forums for print on demand photo books. There are also good reviews of *myphotobook.co.uk, smilebooks.com, yophoto.co.uk, blurb.com, bobbooks.co.uk* and *lulu.com*. Some are not based in the UK, so do check delivery costs.

Most photo book publishers offer free downloads of their own template layout software, which allows you choose book sizes, hardback or paper-back, finishes and templates for layouts, into which you drop your pictures and text. Most POD companies also offer calendars, diaries, books you can write in (recipes, gardening and holiday journals for example). There are annual awards for the best photo books, run by Blurb.

ISBN and Barcodes for Books

If you produce a book just for family and friends and/or as a marketing tool, you do not need an ISBN (International Standard Book Number). However, if you want to get a book printed which can be sold on Amazon and other internet stores and which people can order through bookshops, you will need an ISBN and barcode.

To buy ISBNs see *www.nielsonbook.co.uk*, the official ISBN site. The minimum you can buy is 10 ISBNs at a cost of £118.68 (2011 prices). Change the format, for example, from hardback to paperback, and you will need a second ISBN. You have to set yourself up as a publisher to get them, but that usually means just having a name—you do not have to be a limited company.

Buy your own ISBN numbers–some POD services offer to supply you with one and the barcode for the back cover, but you have more control if you own the ISBN.

Print on Demand Books

These companies offer print on demand services for books and calendars etc., but are geared towards the self-publisher who also wants to sell their books. Lulu and CreateSpace are popular POD publishing services in North America, but as books are usually dispatched from there, postage costs for European buyers can be very expensive. For a good print-on-demand and publishing solution in the UK, Lightning Source is among the most popular. It is also used by traditional publishing companies.

Some print on demand services offer cover and page design templates but these may not suit what you want. If you are not adept at book design, you will need a book designer. In the UK, it can cost a great deal for a professional book designer, depending on the extent and complexity of your intended book. You could post the project asking for a designer on *www.peopleperhour.com* or *www.freelancer.co.uk* or other sites where you can ask people to bid and you will get bids from around the world that will be a lot cheaper. The book designer need not be in the UK but do check out their expertise and do all you can (feedback, internet searches etc) to ensure they are bona fide.

POD companies like Lightning Source (as opposed to printers of photo books) will also distribute the books for you, meaning that if you have an ISBN and someone orders your book, whether from Amazon or a bookshop, the order will go through to the printing company and they will print and dispatch it for you. Of course, they take a cut for this service. The customer usually pays postage, on top of the retail price. Every online shop from which your book is ordered will also want its cut.

While physical bookshops will rarely stock self-published books, if someone walks in and wants a copy, having an ISBN means the bookshop can order it for them. You might persuade your local bookshop to stock some as they do like supporting local authors/artists. They will demand a wholesale price (usually between 35-60% off your retail price), and will also ask for sale or return, so if the books don't sell, they can return them to you.

Print on demand has been criticised for low quality for reproducing photographs but has improved immeasurably in recent years. As technology advances, the quality is getting better. Colour is still expensive for POD but is likely to get cheaper in future.

If you go the self-publishing route, you will also be responsible for marketing the book. Some self-publishing firms offer a marketing service for a fee, but do check forums to see if there are happy or unhappy customers of such marketing services. There are also some companies which offer purely marketing services. However, most photographers will better know the market for their book. Marketing takes time and determination, so only take it on if you can do the book justice. If your book is on Amazon or other online retailer, get as many people as you can to review it. You can send free review copies with a press release (see Chapter Five, Marketing) to appropriate magazines and newspapers and websites, although be aware that many newspapers and magazines won't review a self-published title.

You could also make your book available as an ebook. Kindle Direct and Smashwords, for example, allow you to publish ebooks for free, in return for a royalty. Ebooks, unlike paper books, are subject to VAT.

Chapter Ten

Stock and Microstock Libraries

here are two main types of image libraries, stock libraries and microstock libraries. Both have millions of photographs. Buyers of photography either go for Rights Managed (RM) or Royalty Free (RF). Rights Managed means they buy a certain usage, often for a certain time and territory. Royalty Free means the photos are sold for any usage but the buyer does not usually get any exclusivity. Although it tends to be microstock libraries which are royalty free, selling rights for any use for peanuts, some RM stock libraries now do both.

Within RM stock libraries, there are generalists collections covering every subject under the sun. There are also hundreds of specialist stock libraries concentrating on, for example, aerial photography, food, travel, weather or wildlife photography—you name it, there is a library specialising in photographs of that subject. A few stock libraries started by photographers sell only his or her own collection, and might not be interested in handling the work of others. Others have started out as a photographer's collection but gone on to become big libraries in their own right, selling work of other photographers as well.

Some stock libraries give guidelines as to the subject matter that is most in demand which are often posted on their sites, on their Facebook pages and on Twitter. They may say they already have over a million sunset photos but very few of snow. They may have more than enough food shots but not enough of teenage boys. They may have millions of London but too few of Lyme Regis. Study the requirements.

Stock libraries all vary slightly as to the technical requirement of size, RGB or CYMK, rights, exclusivity arrangements and the commission they take. You may have to search a bit on their sites, or search using the name of the agency/stock library with 'submission guidelines'. As most agency and stock library websites are there to attract buyers; advice for contributing photographers may be hidden away.

Some agencies/libraries even have a list of cameras from which they will only accept pictures. With a few, this is quite restricted to top end dslrs, usually Canon and Nikon. It could influence your future choice of camera.

Many stock libraries ask you to submit a few photos before they approve you as a contributor. Comments on forums reveal that many really good photographers are rejected on the first go, so it is worth trying again. Some stock libraries have time limits before you can submit again. For any submission, make sure you include your name as you want it to appear as a credit. You may need to submit a caption and signed model or property release where needed. You will certainly have to know about keywording. Most stock libraries offer advice on their sites. There are also specialist companies offering keywording services and there is some keywording software available, (see Microstock), especially for stock photographers.

You should also read the guidelines of trademarks—most stock libraries will not accept a photo showing a trade mark. This is not just the brand names and logos we all know about; you can take and submit to stock libraries a day light photo of the Eiffel Tower: you cannot sell one of it at night, unless a general Paris landscape, as the lights are trade marked.

One of the biggest stock libraries, Alamy (*www.alamy.com*), has around 25 million photos, and adds around 15,000 new images per day. Alamy takes around 40% commission. Getty Images, another huge library that has been swallowing lots of smaller fish, has several options: they sell stock, sell stock under the brands of other libraries they have bought, and act as a news press agency as well. It likes images with good composition, good lighting and a strong concept, rather than story telling. Crops and lighting should both enhance a subject, avoiding busy or cluttered backgrounds. Getty Images says it likes photography that communicates as a metaphor, such as growth, tenderness, teamwork, tranquillity etc. It is less strict than some on the camera used but it must be a dslr, with RAW or uncompressed TIFF images of the highest quality.

The main general stock libraries include Alamy, Corbis, Getty (owner of Jupiter Images, amongst others), Aurora Photos and Masterfile (also owner of Crestock microstock). Press agencies also have stock libraries.

Photographers Direct (*www.photographersdirect.com*) is also popular, especially as it only takes 20% commission but it won't accept photographers who market any work through microstock libraries. Photographers Direct operates slightly differently from other stock libraries. You upload a low resolution photo to its website for buyers to see and if they buy, you then negotiate usage fees direct with the buyers. Its website says the average fee is about $200 so, less the 20% commission, you would receive $160. It also says that images have fetched up to $5000. Compare this to the few cents you will receive for the same image if sold through microstock and you can see why it is popular with professional photographers.

Uploading to stock and microstock libraries is time consuming. Some photographers employ an assistant to do it for them.

To find stock libraries,

> www.bapla.org.uk
>
> www.stockindexonline.com
>
> www.stockartistsalliance.org
>
> www.visualconnections.com
>
> www.cepic.org, (lists members in 20 countries)
>
> www.selling-stock.com (subscription based)

Microstock

Microstock photography companies source and sell their images almost exclusively via the Internet. They do so from a wider range of photographers than the traditional stock agencies, including from amateurs. They usually sell their images at a very low rate (anywhere from a few pence to say £10–20) for a royalty free image. A number of microstock sites also sell vector, Flash animations and video.

Most microstock libraries have millions of photographs to sell, covering every conceivable subject. However, a popular photo can sell many times as buyers are rarely after exclusive rights.

All microstock libraries take a percentage of each sale (some take just 30%, others 60%, depending which contributor package you opt for), and set a threshold limit that you have to meet in sales before they pay you anything. As most microstock sites are American, this is usually $50 or $100.

They will also ask you to pick key words for each image so when people search using key words, your photo has a better chance of coming up. Some sites have good zoom facilities that allow customers to see your photograph in detail.

Each microstock library's submission guidelines vary slightly. You may need to upload thousands of images before you start earning. As with RM stock, you must also ensure that no logos, brands or patented technologies or designs are infringing copyright and trademark law. Photos of identifiable people or property will need model or property release forms.

Pay attention to the technical specs demanded for the photographs you download. Too small, too light or dark, too much noise and you might find your photos rejected.

If you go the microstock route, it can be worth registering with more than one microstock agency, as you are not obliged to stick with just one, or even to restrict one photograph to one microstock agency, although with some, you can sign exclusive agreements usually in return for a slightly higher percentage. Obviously, the more photographs you have on each, the better your chances of selling some.

You may also find that some of the photographs you thought odd or boring sell the most. On forums of the microstock sites, one photographer said that his picture of a man dressed as a rabbit on a motorbike had sold well, while another said his boring photographs of street signs had sold most.

You may not get a credit line and you will have little control over how your pictures are used, cropped or altered. Most microstock sites also offer additional income from referrals to both buyers and contributors.

Don't expect a massive income though—very few photographers make a living from microstock. Yuri Arcurs is reputed to earn around $1.3 million a year with microstock but he is definitely the exception. His website, *www. arcurs.com*, is worth reading. Not only does he generously give advice on the microstock business but technical advice on why many photos are rejected. This advice is equally applicable to main (macro) stock libraries. He also offers a popular keywording tool plus reports on his sales to each of the main microstock libraries.

Uploading can take some time and many photographers don't think it is worthwhile for the amounts they receive in payments.

The main microstock libraries are listed here, although others are springing up all the time or being gobbled up by larger stock libraries.

> BigStockPhoto
> www.bigstockphoto.com
> BigStock was acquired by Shuttercock but still operates under its own brand.

> CanStockPhoto
> www.canstockphoto.com
> Canadian based microstock agency

> Dreamstime
> www.dreamstime.com
> Popular choice for European customers.

FeaturePics
www.featurepics.com
FeaturePics is not strictly a microstock agency as it is you who sets the picture price. Featurepics gives photographers 70% of the sale price.

Fotolia
www.en.fotolia.com
New York based but with a large number of European users.

iStockPhoto
www.istockphoto.com
Owned by Getty Images, istockphoto is perhaps the biggest name in stock photography.

Shutterstock
www.shuttercock.com
American based but used by British photographers.

123RF
www.123rf.com
A microstock library based in the UK. The RF stands for Royalty Free.

Others include StockXpert, Crestock (owned by Masterfile) and Veer.

Chapter Eleven

Setting Up A Studio

*D*o you really need a studio? If your work is all fashion, packshots and food, then probably you do. However, studios eat into budgets, so it may be worth hiring one for each shoot, and not worrying about the monthly rent, rates etc.

Before committing to a studio, there are various things to consider:

1. Location—do you need to be in the centre of town?
2. Will clients be visiting you?
3. Do you need to impress? If so, a nice area, convenient for transport/with parking and a studio in good order (or made so) will be prerequisite.
4. Do you need passing trade, and therefore good footfall? Do you need frontage to the street?
5. If you have your eye on a premises, has it the right licence for a studio? The landlord/council can advise on licences and a change of use may be allowed. Studios are classified as B1.

What size studio do you need? Once you have set up cameras on tripods, lights, backdrops, it may be more than you think. How much storage space? What is the light like—is that important? Are there enough power points? Is there somewhere for models to change?

You will need buildings insurance, although it depends how you rent—if you are just renting a space within someone else's studio, the rent may cover insurance and extras. Rent or lease full time and you will have to pay insurance. There may also be service charges to pay. The landlord will probably also charge VAT, which, unless you are VAT registered and can claim back, will add to your bill.

If you take on a lease and then want to leave early, unless you have a 'get out' (break) clause in the contract, you could find yourself liable for paying rent, rates and service charges for the full lease term. Your contract may also say that you cannot then sublet to help defray these costs. Even if you can sublet, if your tenant defaults on payments, you may still be liable for the rent for the whole term of the lease.

Some leases are 'full-repairing', meaning you have to restore the property back to the state it was when the very first lease was first issued. As this might have been decades ago, you may find yourself with a hefty repair bill. There is sometimes a premium to pay for buying a lease, on top of rent, although with so many empty commercial properties around, it is less common unless the property is in a prime position. If you do go for a lease, make sure the premises are correctly classified for use as a studio, usually B1, or can be reclassified. The landlord and local council will tell you.

If the public or employees will be on site, you need public liability insurance. You also need insurance for your camera gear/laptop etc. Do you have, or can you afford all the equipment you need? You may need to install a phone and broadband. You will also need excellent security, especially if you intend leaving camera gear there overnight. You also need fire precautions, which may mean putting in fire doors, smoke alarms etc. The Fire Brigade is happy to advise on this.

Obviously, you need to make sure there is at least one toilet and basin that you and guests/employees can use, even if it is shared with others in the building. If you intend to employ people, there are various health and safety requirements as well.

Again, it is worth have a business plan, with income projections, to see if a studio is viable. You will certainly need a business plan if you need to raise any money from banks and other funders. For legal responsibilities of renting and leasing and for business plans, see *www.businesslink.gov.uk*.

Artists and photographers often form collectives, where they take over a building or floor and may also rent space out to others. Often, these are part-funded by an arts' organisations, charities and/or councils.

Your local council will often have studios for rent, or look at local classified forums. Studios and space sharing often feature on:

www.photographers.co.uk

www.artshub.co.uk

www.workspacegroup.co.uk

www.acme.org.uk

www.creativeprocess.org.uk

www.gumtree.com

www.rentscheme.co.uk

www.rentmystudio.co.uk

www.movethat.co.uk

You could also buy an existing studio business. Often, you are buying not only the lease/freehold premises but goodwill, (reputation, brand, client list) and equipment. However, if the studio is known for rather old-fashioned portraits, it may be hard to change the image to sell your style or to change from say, portraits to products. On the other hand, it can mean you can set up quickly. The studio may be fully equipped, which may prove cheaper than buying new or even second hand but do ensure it is right for the sort of work you want to do. There may be good existing photo management software and accounts software packages included in the sale.

The owner may well offer, or be obliged as part of the sale agreement, to stay on for a handover period, or act as a consultant for a certain amount of time. It is worth getting an independent business valuation, not just one for the premises. Your accountant should be able to help or can introduce you to a business valuer. Never just take the word of the seller or his/her agent. You and your accountant should also look at the filed accounts. Don't fall for the owner's line that profits are really much greater as most of the business is cash-in-hand and not in the accounts.

One photographer told me how he expanded his studio photography business. He was doing so well with one that he leased three more studios in other towns. He spent his entire time finding and managing staff, driving between studios and hadn't picked up his camera for weeks. Not only that, he was making less money for himself. His turnover had increased but after costs of rent, staff and other overheads, the actual profits went substantially down. He was also frustrated and unhappy—he hadn't wanted to be a manager. He was a photographer. In the end, he sold the three studios as going concerns, and even made a profit. He kept the first studio and became a photographer again.

If you are selling a business as a going concern (for photographers, this usually means a studio or photo library), it is worth planning well in advance. Doing a big push for business for at least the three years before you sell can increase the price you ask.

Chapter Twelve

Exhibiting Your Work

Most photographers would like to exhibit their work and there are hundreds of galleries in the UK that either specialise in photographic work or have occasional group or one-man photographic shows. Some will run an occasional open exhibition, which most photographers can enter, although the terms and conditions may stipulate only photographers from a limited geographic region or in a certain age group.

Most top London galleries, such as Chris Beetles Gallery, will invite top photographers to exhibit and usually won't consider anyone who is not a 'name'. The National Portrait Gallery and other public galleries are also highly unlikely to consider exhibiting or buying your work if you have not already made a name for yourself, although the National Portrait Gallery does show the annual Taylor Wessing competition finalists.

There are smaller galleries around the country that are willing to consider lesser known photographers and they may be open to suggestions of an exhibition, particularly if it has a theme that is either relevant to their location and to their philosophy. Many galleries do like work on a theme, rather than a random set of photographs but if your work is good enough, they may consider a one-man show or a space within a collective show.

Of course, galleries are not the only place to exhibit you work. Cafes, restaurants, libraries, antique and gift shops, shopping centres, club premises, hotels, sports centre, community spaces, theatre and concert room foyers, also exhibit work of artists and photographers. Some company reception areas may also consider exhibiting your work, although there could be security considerations of allowing the public into their buildings.

The Advantages of Exhibiting

Apart from a major boost to your ego, having your work exhibited is good for your cv, increases your visibility and can enhance your reputation (and therefore, hopefully, your prices for future work). The main advantage is the PR that can surround an exhibition and a good gallery will mail the press and appropriate websites for you. Local papers, magazines, TV and radio may pick up on it. Galleries will also invite the press to your opening.

The gallery should also have a mailing list of buyers: it will send them details of your show and an invitation to an opening event. You will also be able to invite existing clients and anyone you think will be a buyer or useful contact in future. There is no guarantee they—or anyone else–will come, even if tempted by a free glass of wine and a cheese straw. Some galleries may ask you to contribute to the cost of refreshments, mailings, invites etc.

PR for Non-Gallery Venues

With non-gallery venues, the PR is usually down to you, although theatres, hotels etc., may have a press officer who will do the PR or help you. You need to send a press release and photo from the show to the local press, local arts and family magazines, local radio and TV, and to listings pages in publications (a second release to the listings editor is a good idea, even to the same newspaper) and on the web. If it is a major venue, also include the national press. Remember deadlines for the press—a monthly magazine covering your county may well want material two months in advance. Send one of the best photographs as well, although do not expect to be paid for its use. It's free publicity. Remember to offer yourself for interview to all press to talk about your work.

If you really don't know where to start with PR, invite bids for a PR expert on *www.peopleperhour.com*, *www.freelancer.co.uk*, or *www.elance.com*. Ask for a fixed fee for a one-off project. It is worth getting someone reasonably local, so they can attend opening events.

Invitations to Exhibition Openings

Create a database of potential clients, sponsors and press contacts, so you can send them an invitation to an opening event. Most people prefer printed invitation, which tend to be better remembered than emails. Have a visitors' book at the exhibition, asking for email addresses. Under the Data Protection Act, you must let people know how you intend to use their contact details and allow them to opt out of receiving communications from you.

Invite art/photography reviewers from the press, not forgetting radio and local television. You do not just want reviewers from photographic magazines: lovely though it is to see your show featured, it will rarely bring you more work. You need to invite existing clients (it is said that it costs eights time more to get a new client than to keep an existing one), and potential clients. It is a good excuse to send an unsolicited mailing to prospective contacts, as no-one will object to being invited to an exhibition. They may not come, of course, but they may pass it on to someone else so creating a potential network referral. Who you invite depends on your field of photography, of course. As with any marketing campaign, the more targeted you invitation list, the better. If you have too many people to invite for one grand opening have two, on consecutive evenings: one for press, main contacts and sponsors, one for family, friends and secondary contacts. It depends how many people you want to invite, on the size of the venue and budgets.

Funding

You may be able to get sponsorship from a local business. Local businesses (e.g. wine merchants, cafes, restaurants etc) may also supply wine or food in return for a mention on your invitations, posters and press releases. A printer or framer may give you a discount in return for a credit. If you get sponsorship, keep the sponsor fully up-to-date. Always delivery what you have promised, in terms of credits, invitations, etc. Ensure you invite anyone who has helped put the exhibition on, supplied free goods, etc., to the opening.

Always discuss with the gallery or venue what you are doing in terms of sponsorship and marketing (if a proper gallery, you will be given a contract), so it doesn't conflict with any sponsorship deals they may have. Although funding for the arts has been cut, your local council may have community/arts funding available for small projects. It is always worth checking out. Some charities may also offer funding, although they usually want any exhibition/project to have a social benefit.

Hiring Galleries

If you need to pay to hire a gallery, determine what is and is not included, as those extras can add up. However, artists are often wary of self-hire venues, as it implies that no professional gallery will exhibit their work. Likewise, collectors do not always like them and they are often ignored by the press. It is best to avoid taking out loans to hire venues.

You might work in a group to spread the costs. It needn't be all photographers: it could be with a sculptor, painter, installation artist, potter etc. You could agree to one group show or even a one man show each for say 1-2 weeks each.

While exhibiting within a group can be a good idea, it is also not without potential problems. Disputes over finances, who has what space, who should be there to oversee visitors–it can all lead to arguments. It is important to have a simple agreement, which you all sign, stating you are all equally liable for all financial and legal arrangements for X period of time. It is wise to agree in writing who will be there and for how long each day to oversee visitors, handle money etc.

It might be worth organising an exhibition space yourself, and then inviting others to participate, for a fee: you remain in charge but get your costings right and you could end up with a free exhibition space for yourself within a group show. You may even make a small profit.

Do find out whether you have to pay insurance and rates for the time you are on any exhibition premises. You will certainly need public liability insurance, although the landlord may cover you under his insurance policy. You may have to sign a document/contract, guaranteeing you will vacate the premises by a certain date.

If selling, as well as showing, consider how you take payments. You may not be able to hire a point of sale card reader for a short time, so will you take cheques? Fewer and fewer people now use them and they could bounce. Know the location of your nearest cash point. It is advisable to always have two people responsible for the exhibition at any one time. Make sure money is kept locked up in a fixed place, not just a portable cash box.

Pop-up Galleries

One increasingly popular way to create an exhibition space is to create a pop-up gallery. It might be an empty shop or industrial building where the owner (sometimes the local council) has given you permission for to use it, often for free, as a gallery for a set period of time—perhaps up to a month. In return, the landlord is given a credit in all publicity material and invited to any opening events. Your local Council can tell you who owns empty properties.

As well as knowing about council-owned properties, council arts officers can often refer artists to non-traditional venues, sympathetic local developers or companies and local community group with which to collaborate. Arts officers often have an ongoing working relationship with local planners, so can also advise artists planning temporary public events. If the council helps find you a venue, you may be able to sell work without paying commission. Do ask if you are allowed to sell work and, if you are having any sort of event, about appropriate license for serving or selling alcohol.

Many such spaces may need decorating and need new lighting. You may be responsible for all aspects of health and safety (especially fire risk) and need public liability and premises insurance, even if only for a few weeks. Check with the landlord—they may be already covered or agree to cover you for free.

Sizes

A3 and A4 are popular sizes as most venue spaces are not huge although prints of these sizes will, of course, need larger mounts and frames. Too big and you may not only have problems displaying work but you may diminish the potential number of buyers. Few people have large amounts of spare wall space at home. A3 invariably costs more than twice A4 to produce, if you take into account framing, printing etc. You need to allow enough space around the framed photographs to allow each to stand out. Too many photos on a wall can lessen their impact. Every photo should have its own short caption card adjacent on the wall.

Set a Theme

Themed photography exhibitions usually work better than a scatter gun approach. A photograph of the wilds of Scotland may look out of place in exhibition of photos of some fashion, some sport.

Pricing

People buy photographs for many reasons: they just like it; they think one day you will be very famous so it's also an investment; it will make an ideal birthday present for their aunt; it goes with their colour scheme. You can price it low as an impulse buy; you can hit the middle market so it shows you value your work and so should they; you can hit the top end, although very expensive photos tend to be by big names exhibiting in top venues. Few people will pay more than £100-200 for an amazing photo (large and framed) by an unknown. Don't price your work so high it is out of reach of your intended market or so low that neither you or potential buyers value it or you fail to at least cover your costs

At business school you are told 'the right price is the most you can get'. Visiting other exhibitions will give you some guidelines. An exhibition of Eve Arnold's photographs at the Chris Beetle's Gallery had prices up to £30,000, although they were for shots of Marilyn Monroe. A gallery in the Midlands has some great framed 6 x 9 photos for sale by local photographers for £35.

Modern art photography has been somewhat devalued by digital, and not everyone considers it an investment, a reason many buy art photography. However, photographers do find a market of digital limited edition and fine art prints.

The price you set depends on many factors: quality, subject, size, whether you are selling your work as art and whether it is a limited edition. If you want to go really commercial, landscapes, city and seascapes, wildlife, flowers and abstracts are more commercial than a shot of an unknown person, although photographs of famous people can add a premium.

Some photographers produce simple decorative pieces. Think of Ikea posters. Others have turned their photos to black and white, changing, with software, one item to colour (like a red balloon or red postbox), printed them on canvas and sold them into shops, unframed. Popular in tourist shops and general interior furnishing stores, these retail at around £40-50.

It is a good guideline to set your retail price at least three to four times your cost price, so you cover costs and make a profit. Costs include printing, framing, business (A5) cards, price lists, hiring an electric cable detectors (essential if hanging the exhibition yourself), spirit level, visitors' book, glass cleaner, wire, tape, caption cards, red dot stickers for sales. If the venue demands commission, you need to factor it in to your costs. Don't forget that most established galleries will add VAT to the retail price.

If a gallery asks you for a fixed price, you need to determine the price at which they will retail your work—it could be a vast markup that gives you very little and them a lot. If your costs are £20 a framed print, your price to the gallery should be at least double, if not more. If they say they will retail each piece for £100, this gives them £60 profit. You could try and sell for say £50, so they have a decent mark-up, but so do you. You make £30, they make £50. You could try £60-70 but be prepared to drop.

Commission Paid To Galleries

Almost all venues will want a commission on sales. Some big commercial London galleries charge as much as 60%. One has been reported as charging 80%.. Before you mutter 'Scandalous! Never!' do bear in mind that London and city centre galleries have huge overheads in rent, rates and staff. They can also charge a lot more for work, reach collectors and buyers that you probably have never heard of, and get more press coverage than you could probably manage. The press is more likely to attend openings at big venues.

Remember, even if you only get 20-30%, it is more than 0% if you can't reach the market. They will also handle the sale, take payments, ship etc.

Even non-gallery spaces, like craft or coffee shops, may want 25-35% (maybe even 40-50%) of your selling price. Some venues may charge a hanging fee of £20-30 per show or higher per month, plus a commission percentage, often around 20-25%, of the sale price. However, shop owners/sales assistants will also be there when the venue is open, and may be prepared to oversee visitors, so you don't have to sit there all day, every day. Usually they will also handle any sales, (retailers invariably have the ability to take credit and debit cards), passing on the agreed percentage to you.

You could also try selling postcards and mounted but unframed prints of exhibited and other works at the venue. You should have a price list, not just for the works on display but perhaps in different sizes, framed and unframed (but all should have mounts). You will also need clear cello bags for unframed prints. Make sure you have a good stock of your postcards or A5 cards for people to take.

Limited Editions

You could offer limited edition prints (from film, colour or black and white). If one limited edition in the exhibition sells, someone might just buy another direct from your price list or website. Do sign and number your work on the mount—it proves its provenance, its limited edition status and people like the personal touch.

For limited editions, put the number on the lower left hand of the mount, with your signature on the right, preferably in pencil. For instance, print number three out of a run of 25 prints is written as 3/25. Print, sign and date a certificate authenticating it to go with the print. If you produce a limited edition, ensure you archive the negative/transparency forever or even destroy it. For digital limited edition, you have to archive the photograph (and any very similar photos) or even delete it.

Cheap Framing

One of the major costs of putting on any exhibition is the framing. You may be able to buy cheap frames at companies like Ikea, Matalan etc, but make sure they are in proportion to the print size you are using- many are based on old 35mm ratios. Pound shops occasionally have rather good frames, and if you chat up your local framer, they may have some from an uncollected order that they will sell you cheaply. Some photographers go to local auctions to buy framed prints, and then reuse the frame. There are also online stores that offer frames for less, although the postage may negate any savings.

If using a picture framer for bespoke frames, try to negotiate a discount–for bulk or because you are a local artist or student. It is always worth asking.

If selling framed prints, always use acid free museum board. It can be worth learning to mount and frame your own pictures. It can even lead to a business opportunity framing for others.

Your professional association may recommend framers/mount suppliers and most reputable photographic sites have lists of suppliers. *www.cotswold-mounts.co.uk, www.cartersmounts.co.uk* and *www.mapleframing.co.uk* have all been recommended on photography forums as has Mount Solutions, which sells on its eBay store.

Why should a non-gallery exhibit your work?

Your exhibition can draw in more customers to his shop/restaurant/wine bar etc.

It's good to entertain existing customers.

The client looks good supporting local artists.

It won't cost him anything.

The local press will probably cover the exhibition, and therefore he gets free publicity too.

He can earn extra money, through a hanging fee and/or commission on sales.

It enhances the décor.

Chapter Thirteen

Law and the Photographer

Copyright, fair use, moral rights, employment, street photography and the Prevention of Terrorism Act, defamation, privacy, trespass, late payment rights, Human Rights Act, EU law—for photographers, the law is a potential minefield. These laws are fiendishly complicated which is why there are many successful law firms that specialise in media law. One of the major advantages of belonging to a union or association like the NUJ or AoP is the legal advice they offer their members.

It is beyond the scope of this book to give specific legal advice (fat books have been written just on copyright law). However, if you are not a member of a professional association or union, there is plenty of free advice available. The websites of major law firms like *www.simkins.co.uk, www.carter-ruck. com, www.out-law.com, www.swan-turton.com, www.withersworldwide.com* and many others have articles on various aspects of the law and photography. Some of these articles have appeared in photography magazines. The Association of Photographers (*www.the-aop.com*) offers excellent advice, as does the American Society of Media Photographers (*www.asmp.org*).

There have been demonstrations, heated discussions and much disquiet over potential curbs on photography by clauses in the Prevention of Terrorism Act. The excellent site 'I'm a Photographer, Not a Terrorist', *www.photographernotaterrorist.org*, gives very clear advice on police powers and updates on amendments to The Prevention of Terrorism Act and also has a 'bust sheet' with advice and your rights.

The police and security guards have very limited powers and cannot confiscate cameras or demand you delete pictures without a court order. Members of the media do not need a permit to photograph in public places, although they must not obstruct traffic or pedestrians, for example, or block exits and entrances, or cause a public nuisance.

The Association of Chief Police Officers has re-issued guidance to police about dealing with the media after a police sergeant recently made a freelance photographer delete images from her camera. It is suggested that you always challenge anyone to name the law they are acting under and then show them the printout 'bust sheet' of your rights.

Defamation

The site of leading law firm, Carter Ruck, has an excellent article on defamation, with examples of cases brought by clients protesting that an image damaged their reputation as it had been manipulated by software, or they were wrongly identified in the caption.

There is also advice on how to protect your own reputation, especially in the internet age. For example, if you receive negative comments on your work on bulletin boards, it may just be fair criticism. On the other hand, if it is vindictive and loses you work, you may have a case against the person who posted the comments. It also suggests that if you do receive negative comments, counteract by posting as many positive comments as possible on bulletin boards and forums, Twitter, Facebook, LinkedIn, etc., to help push any negative pages down in an internet search. You could also sign up for a service like Google Alert, so you receive emails of any mentions of your name.

There are also some organisations that offer free legal advice, although much is limited to offering *pro bono* advice (free for the public good) to the disadvantaged. But it is worth a try. The Citizens Advice Bureau, *www.citizensadvice.org.uk* is probably more used to housing claims but may direct you to a specialist who will advise for free. You could also try *www.lawworks.org.uk, www.lawcentres.org.uk,* and *www.cantaffordalawyer.org.*

Lawyers also give regular free advice sessions at Toynbee Hall, London, *www.toynbeehall.org.uk* but you are unlikely to get a specialist. You might, if employed, have access to a free legal advice service (your employment contract should tell you, or ask the HR department). Depending on your buildings, home and camera insurance supplier, you may also have access to free legal advice helpline. Access to legal advice can be one of the many benefits of belonging to a professional photographers' association.

Working with Children and Vulnerable Adults

If you work as, for example, a schools' photographer or are documenting a year in the life of a care home, you may need a Criminal Records Bureau check, which can take a month or so to receive. The self-employed can't apply for a CRB check themselves but can ask the school or an agency, such as photo library, to apply for them.

If it is just a one-off job, you should not need one although you may need the Vetting and Barring Scheme approval, run by the CRB, under the auspices of the Independent Safeguarding Authority, ISA: *www.isa-gov.org.uk*.

The system is, hopefully, more relaxed concerning photography. Don't be taken in by the many sites on the web which say you need a CRB and offer to get one for you, for a fee. Current fees for the different levels of checks, an Enhanced CRB, Standard CRB or a VBS/ISA (Independent Safeguarding Authority check) are published on *www.direct.gov.uk* or telephone 0870 9090811.

Even if only for your portfolio, always ask permission from the parents before photographing children. There have been reports of photographers being beaten up for taking photos of children in parks. If you want to use the photos for any commercial reason, a minor's model release form is a must.

Respect Other Cultures

In certain cultures, even within the UK, a woman may not be alone with a man who is not related. Although not determined by the law in the UK, it can be in other countries or at least so culturally unacceptable you are asking for trouble. Similarly, in some cultures a female photographing a man will be difficult.

Contracts—Devils in the Detail

Contracts sometimes include clauses that indemnify the client against the consequences of their use of the photographer's work. Never, ever sign a contract with such a clause. It might seem innocent now but can come back to haunt you. Your innocent advertising or editorial photos inadvertently contains a brand/trade mark that is clearly visible. The owners of the brand could claim the context of the use of the photo brings their brand into disrepute. They could then sue your client, who in turn can sue you.

Photographers should also insert a clause in their own contracts (or ensure it is in the one they receive from a client) stating that no rights at all are sold until their invoice is paid in full. This helps with getting paid but also prevents third parties buying a bankrupt client's assets—including rights to a photographer's pictures—but not their obligations, such as paying the photographer for these rights.

Most commissioning clients will have their own contracts. However, if the terms and conditions in it are unfavorable, explain you just cannot sign it as it is and ask for the clauses to be removed, (struck out and signed by the client). Similarly, if the client tries to renegotiate terms after the commission, you should make it clear, nicely but firmly, that you have a contract, and you should not agree to new terms unless you are happy to do so. You could also try and renegotiate the fee to terms acceptable to you.

Clients may also use purchase orders, also with terms and conditions, which may be used instead of, or as well as, a contract but with different terms. Read these carefully and do not quote the purchase order on an invoice unless you agree to the terms, even if you already have a contract. It could indicate that you accept the new terms.

If you are paid by cheque, with wording on the back of the cheque that all or other rights are transferred to the client and asking you to sign it on the back, simply strike out the wording. It has no case under UK law. To be on the safe side, write to the client saying the cheque has been received for xx rights originally sold.

Many magazines and newspaper publishers use a self-billing system and do not make clear their terms and conditions and the rights they are paying for. Do ask upfront for terms and conditions, as accepting a payment by this system could indicate you agree to their terms which may not be favourable to you. You could inadvertently give away rights.

Model Releases—Vitally Important Forms

Many photographers will need model and property releases if they are to sell their work for publication or as stock. The exception is usually for news pictures and most photojournalism/editorial use. You need:

1. Adult model releases (for people over 18)
2. Minor model releases
3. Property releases
4. Art releases

Model releases have become increasingly important in protecting photographers in an age when lawyers offer no-win, no-fee services, and the public sees a chance to sue and get damages for defamation of character, invasion of privacy etc., through the photograph's use of an image or the way a publication uses it. No stock library will accept identifiable models for commercial use without a model release.

It's fine to take pictures of family and friends or anyone that can be identified, if you have their consent. It's not fine to sell those pictures to a stock library or advertising agency without a signed model release form. You could also hit problems if your picture of someone in the street is published altered or distorted or adversely captioned, resulting in defamation–damage to their reputation.

Even most modern fine art needs a release form signed by the artist or copyright owner of the piece, unless it is in a public place. In some countries, even if the art work is in a public place, a published photograph can infringe the copyright of the artist.

You can take a photo of a building and sell it if the photo was taken from a public place. You can't usually sell it without a signed property release if you were on the premises. If photographing children, you need a minor's model release, signed by a legal guardian (usually a parent). Children who are professional models need to be licensed, so always use a reputable model agency.

There are many template model releases published on the web, all with rather different wording according to the legal jurisdiction in which they are issued. Agencies such as Getty Images and Alamy have templates you can download. The Association of Photographers is among the associations that also offer free downloads of model releases. The wording of these model releases will cover you in most jurisdictions. Photographers are advised to always carry copies of each and to get them signed if in any doubt. They are for your own protection. You need three copies for each shoot or set of pictures (not one for each shot): one for you, one for the model or parent, property owner or artist, and one for your client, whether it's a publication, press agency or stock library.

Chapter Fourteen

Licenses and Copyright

*T*he majority of photographers never sell the copyright in their photographs. What you, the photographer, sells is reproduction rights under licence, and under the Copyright Designs and Patents Act 1988, the copyright of the photograph is yours and remains yours, unless you assign it. That copyright covers any medium—print, the web, film,—everything. Copyright in the UK is for the duration of 70 years from the end of the calendar year in which the creator dies. You cannot copyright ideas, only your interpretation of that idea.

There is a clear distinction between assigning copyright and licensing rights. Assignment means the sale of copyright itself. Licensing means the granting of rights by the creator of the work (i.e. you, the photographer), to use the work for agreed purposes, in agreed ways for an agreed length of time and even in specific territories. You remain the copyright holder. Under UK law copyright holders can only assign copyright in a written document. You are strongly advised never to do so.

It is suggested that some aspects of copyright law in the UK may change. At the time of going to press, any changes had not been announced. However, The Association of Photographers, Red Eye, Pro-Imaging and other photography organisations, *http://artists-bill-of-rights.org* and The Intellectual Property Office, *www.ipo.gov.uk,* will have the latest news on any changes.

There are many different forms of licence. It might be you sell a licence for a photograph for first time UK rights, and for a specified time. This ensures the client some exclusivity within the UK for say, six months or a year. You might sell world rights, for all time, which should cost the client more. Some companies even ask for rights covering the whole universe. You might sell world rights, in all media or confine the licence to print.

It all depends what the client wants to use the photograph for, where and for how long.

Copyright and Commissioned Work

There used to be some confusion over who owned the copyright in commissioned work but this was clarified under the Copyright Designs and Patents Act 1988. It now means that commissioned work remains the copyright of the creator (i.e. you, the photographer).

Your client might say they own the copyright as they have commissioned you and you would never have taken the photographs without them. However, the fee they pay you is for a licence for use, unless you have agreed otherwise. This should be clarified and put in a written contract before the commission begins. You might refer clients to *www.copyright4clients.com,* which aims to educate clients commissioning photography.

It might be the client wants exclusive use of the work they commissioned. They can buy world rights in all media in all territories for all time. You could assign the copyright in full, which needs to be put in writing but you should expect a substantially higher fee. It is not recommended. You have no control over the use of this work or its manipulation and no further payments for its use at any time in the future.

In practice, most commissioned work will be of little further financial use to the photographer. Some photographs might be useful for your portfolio. If you want to put the pictures on your website, it is worth getting your client's permission first. Make sure the photographs are watermarked. No client wants to open a magazine in some far flung country and see the pictures he commissioned you to take, to which neither you and the client agreed.

Reselling commissioned work where you have already sold exclusive rights, for example, is the fastest route to a career serving burgers and fries. You really do not want to upset clients and, depending on the rights you have assigned, they could sue you. You could also be in breach of Trademark law. Even entering a shot in a competition or exhibition can cause legal problems unless you get permission, preferably in writing. If you have sold exclusive world rights to your client, you cannot then put the pictures into a stock library.

However, if the commission is a series of landscapes photographs of the countryside at dawn, you might, depending on the rights the client buys, be able to sell it to another magazine abroad or to a stock library. You should, however, ensure you only resell after any time limit of the licence has expired.

Clients increasingly need–and demand–a wider range of rights, especially as so much now also appears on the web, and these right should be determined from the start.

All commissions and terms of the licence should be in writing. The commissioning client might well have a standard contract. Read the terms and conditions before you sign, to ensure you are not assigning copyright or moral rights to the client unless you are happy to do so. Higher rates or extra fees should always be paid for specialist expertise, exclusivity, web or television use in addition to print, repeat use and any additional press release or other distribution.

Some clients may have small print in a contract that assigns copyright to them, often called 'rights grabbing'. Such small print sometimes appears in purchase orders. Photographers are advised to reject these terms and conditions and not sign the contract nor accept the purchase order. You should put in writing the terms and conditions that you originally agreed, even if only verbatim, with the client.

In the 2010 survey by the British Photographic Council, 72% of photographers who participated said they had encountered a client who thinks that by commissioning a photograph, the copyright belongs to the client. The survey also revealed that freelance photographers who routinely keep their copyright (i.e. by not assigning it) earned on average 33.2% more than those who give it away.

Moral Rights

Moral rights are in addition to copyright but are covered by the same Act in UK law. Moral rights are the right to object if your work is distorted. These rights protect your reputation, the integrity of your work and give you the right to be identified (by an accurate credit line) as the author of the work. In the age of digital manipulation, these rights have become more important—they give you rights if someone uses your work and digitally manipulates it. 'All rights Reserved' or 'Moral Rights Asserted' should be stamped on the back of a print or on a sticker on a photograph or by using the digital equivalent. It should also be put on invoices. Clients may demand (in that small print) that moral rights be waived. This is allowed under UK law but photographers are advised to resist it.

Important exclusions to the Copyright Act

Copyright and Employment

If you are employed as a photographer for a UK company, perhaps working for a newspaper, studio, fashion house, wedding firm etc., the situation is rather different concerning copyright. Under UK law, the copyright in photographs you have taken in the course of your employment belong to your employer. Employees also have no right to a credit line.

Domestic Clients

Studio, wedding and many portrait photographers also need to know about the other exclusion to the Act. This forbids them publishing, broadcasting or exhibiting photographs taken for private domestic clients without the client's permission.

Fair Use/Fair Dealing

The Copyright, Designs and Patents Act 1988 includes certain provisions regarding 'fair dealing', or Fair Use in the USA), which are certain uses of copyright works that do not require the permission of the copyright owner nor infringe the copyright in the original work.

These include: 1. Fair dealing for the purposes of research or private study; 2. Fair dealing for the purposes of criticism or review, whether of the work itself or of another work or performance, provided it is accompanied by sufficient acknowledgement;

Usage would not be considered fair if the usage competes with the normal exploitation of the work. The UK Copyright Service has further details: *www.copyrightservice.co.uk*.

Secondary Rights

If someone prints your work off the web or photocopies it for reference, you are entitled to be paid for what is called 'secondary rights'. To collect such payments, photographers should register with the Design and Artists Copyright Society: *www.dacs.org.uk*. Libraries and press offices, for example, in the UK and abroad, may photocopy your work. These pay DACS a licence fee, which, in turn, pays you.

A Case of Rights' Grabbing.

Photographers should be very careful when uploading photos to some social media sites. Recently, one social network allowed a picture social network the rights to distribute and sell photographers' work to commercial enterprises, such as photo agencies, with no fee to the photographer, despite the fact that the photographer retains the copyright. This is particularly of concern for photos of celebrities or news events, which can have considerable commercial value.

Avoid any site if the terms state something along the lines of:

> *'You retain all ownership rights and copyright to content uploaded to X company. However, by submitting content to X, you hereby grant X (and its successors, subsidiaries, affiliates and any company within its group) a worldwide, non-exclusive, royalty-free, sub-licensable and transferable license to use, reproduce, distribute, prepare derivative works of and display the content in any media formats and through any media channels.'*

They rarely state anything about fees, because there won't be any.

Photographers should always read the terms and conditions of any platform to which they upload their work, to ensure they are not giving away any licensing rights or copyright. The same should be said of all photography competitions. Do not submit work to any organisation, social media, competition, photo sharing site, or other organisation that demands, without payment and permission, any free and unlimited usage, licensing rights or copyright. The American Society of Media Photographers, *www asmp.org*, has an excellent article on photography and the use of social media.

Tracking Usage Of Your Pictures

While the internet has opened up the world for potential sales and marketing opportunities for photographers, it is also open to abuse. It is not difficult to copy work off the web and use it without payment. It helps if your photographs are watermarked, although it does not 100% protect your work.

There is little option on the web other than to display such low resolution pictures they are unlikely to be used for print. In the British Photographic Council Survey 2010, three out of five photographers respondents had had at least one internet copyright infringement.

There are image recognitions software programmes if you think your work might have been used without permission. Most of these offer only a basic free service with enhanced paid-for utilities. There is new software for image searches coming online all the time.

www.tineye.com

www.imagerights.com

www.picscout.com (now owned by Getty)

www.picsearch.com

You can also search for the words you used in your photograph's title, caption and other accompanying text. For example, news (and the date/ place/names); football (and the date/place/names).

It is also worth searching on Google Images, *www.altavista.com/image/ default* and images on other mainstream search engines.

Infringement—Someone Nicked My Photos!

If someone infringes your copyright, such as claiming your work as theirs, using it in print, exhibitions, competitions or on a website, or offers your work for resale, without your, or your agent's or stock library's, permission and payment, you should first inform them in writing that you are the copyright owner. You should ask for an immediate undertaking that they cease from the infringing activities, put them on 'desist and take down' notice and at the same time, ask for their proposal as to payment of damages.

If you do not get a satisfactory response within a very short time, (a few days, a week at most), you could ask your union (e.g. the NUJ if you are a member), your professional association (e.g. the AoP) or even ask a solicitor to send a stern letter threatening legal action and seeking damages. Or you can write a carefully worded letter yourself. Carolyn E Wright, on her website, *www.photoattorney.com*, has a sample letter, which although for American photographers, is equally valid for the UK.

If the case isn't settled out-of-court, you may have no choice but to go to court, which can get very expensive indeed. The Small Claims Court in the UK no longer accept cases of copyright infringement and it is rare to find a law firm who will act for you on a 'no win, no fee' basis.

You could try and find a professional body to which the offending organisation might belong, and complain to them. Most newspapers, magazines and industry sectors belong to a professional organisation.

Takedown Notices

The most common cause for complaints is misuse on, or via, the web. Fortunately for photographers, the Digital Millennium Copyright Act (DMCA) was signed at the 1996 World Intellectual Property Organization (WIPO) Geneva conference. The DMCA states that while an Internet Service Provider (ISP) is not liable for transmitting information that may infringe a copyright, the ISP must remove materials from users' websites that appear to constitute copyright infringement after it receives proper notice.

If you find a website is using one of your images without permission, contact the ISP that is hosting the culpable website to report the infringement and ask that the infringement stop. This letter is called a 'DMCA takedown notice'. The ISP is required to make its agent's name and address available so that you can send it the notification.

To find the hosting ISP, try *www.whois.net*, and *www.domaintools.com/research/dns/*. Another search option is *www.samspade.org*. Also try entering the offending website name and dropping the 'www'.

You can also try the domain name registration databases. Enter the offending domain name in the search box, and then click on the name—it usually tells you who owns it.

You can also copy and paste the URL of the page you have found into *www.archive.org*. This should show you any earlier versions of the offending page. Print them all out.

Your Takedown Notice to the hosting ISP must meet certain requirements. It must be in writing and signed by you, the copyright owner (if you email, your electronic signature is sufficient). You should include low resolution copies of the images that have been used. State that you are complaining in good faith, and, under penalty of perjury, that the information contained in the notification is accurate and that you are the copyright holder of these images. After the ISP receives the notice, it should remove the infringing materials within a reasonable time.

Imitation: The Sincerest Form of Flattery?

If you develop a successful style and someone copies you, be flattered. However, a photographer copying your style is not only trying to steal a bit of your market but may be claiming your creative thought process as his own and being paid for it. If one of your photographs was used, say, for a book cover and you suddenly see a major advertising campaign with almost the same shot (re-taken by someone else), you might have a case for plagiarism.

There have been several cases of photographers complaining that firms, ad agencies and even a major artist, have stolen their image idea. Several cases have made it to court and most have found in favour of the original photographer. You can read some cases on The Editorial Photographers site, *www.epuk.org*.

While going to court can be expensive, threatening to bring a court action can result in compensation being paid before it gets that far. If it does go to court, you might find a lawyer prepared to act on a 'no win, no fee' basis (that doesn't mean that any award is totally yours—the lawyers will take at least 30% if you win.). However, be aware that if the case goes against you, you may still have to pay costs. Your professional association or union may be able to advise.

When starting on the road to a photography career, by all means try and imitate others: it is a very useful way of learning. However, picture editors frequently complain that they see too many photographs in someone else's style. They are not stupid. They can spot a copycat at a hundred paces. Develop your own style.

More information and advice can be found through The Design & Artists Copyright Society, *www.dacs.org.uk* and the Intellectual Property Office, *www.iop.gov.uk*. The AoP also offers legal advice.

Image and database management software for photographers

www.capture.co.uk

www.imagefolio.com

www.scl.co.uk

www.thirdlight.com

www.vision-software.co.uk

www.i-base.com

www.iview-multimedia.com

www.piction.com

www.indexdata.dk

www.greenstone.org

www.infradox.com

www.thedataarchive.com

http://pa.photoshelter.com

www.twensoft.com

www.i-salonsoftware.co.uk

www.frontrange.com

www.momapix.com

www.hindsight.com

www.photobyte.com

www.fotobiz.com

Chapter Fifteen

Rates of Pay

See *www.londonfreelance.org*

Every photographer should look at this site.

This site, the London arm of the NUJ, offers a comprehensive guide to suggested minimum rates for photographers in many different types of media, plus minimum suggested day rates for commissions and post-production work. These rates are, of course, not set in stone but are minimum guidelines from which to negotiate.

The tables of rates include day rates for commissions and stock sales for large circulation magazines, smaller consumer magazines and trade magazines, national and regional newspapers, books, corporate work, online work, public relations work and post-production fees. It suggests 50% be added for simultaneous web publications.

The rates given are for 35mm or DSLR work–rates are usually higher for studio work or large format work. It some cases, such as trade or cheap specialist magazines, for example, the prices are a bit optimistic: £250 for a cover, for example or £100 for half a page. Some trade magazines are now using microstock and paying very little or tapping into enthusiastic amateurs to get photographs for free. On the other hand, suggested minimum fees for corporate work, of day rates starting at £800 to £1500–£2000 a day, plus expenses, reflecting the reputation, talent and skill of the photographer, seems about right.

The guide is primarily for UK media. Fees are often higher in the USA and in major European countries. The site suggests charging 25%–35% more than for equivalent UK publications.

The site does say, about freelancers for national newspapers, for example, that it is no longer possible to earn a professional salary on national day rates without considerable additional sales through syndication, which may never happen and which is also dependent on retaining copyright. However, the guide does not cover the rates for paparazzi, who can earn a small fortune with syndication of the right shot. Remember, tabloid papers invariably pay much more for exclusive pictures than the 'quality' papers (still called broadsheet, although most have reduced their page size).

The NUJ suggests that no photographer should work for less than £250 a day, although the site's rate table puts a minimum day rate of £120 for regional dailies and £100 a day for weekly and local papers. Newspaper magazine supplements often pay more than the newspaper itself.

There is also *www.fotoQuote.com*, a US company, where subscribers access its suggested rates for images for a variety of licenses. It has recently tied up with *www.photoshelter.com* and allows its members access.

Useful websites

www.londonphotographers.org

www.nuj.org.uk

http://media.gn.apc.org

www.nvjphoto.co.uk, (note the v not u);

www.epuk.org

For the USA, The American Association of Media Photographers, www.asmp.org, has examples of real invoices under Paper Share, and the National Press Photographers Association, www.nppa.org, has a fees calculator. Also see www.editorialphoto.com and www.aphotoedit.com

Other useful sites

The Association of Photographers: www.the-aop.org

British Picture Libraries and Agencies: www.bapla.org

Stock Artists Alliance: www.stockartistsalliance.org

British Press Photographers' Association: www.thebppa.com

Commissioned Shoots and Stock

Clients may pay a day rate, half day rate, hour rate or on how the shoot is intended to be used (known as reproduction or repro fees). For print (for magazines, newspapers and books), it may be that the client buyer insists on paying on page rates, i.e. how many photographs are used and at what size within a publication. Sometimes rates are also dictated by print runs (the higher the print run, usually higher the fee), as well as territories (i.e. where the publication is published and sold).

Some photographers, especially those in editorial markets, restrict reproduction rights to one issue of a newspaper or magazine, or may restrict the number of times the image can be used, (i.e. 'one-time' rights).

Some photographers set their day rates as a base fee, with extra payments due for the amount of space the photos take up in the magazines or newspaper. Cover shots for print media are usually charged at a higher rate than work used inside the publication. For billboards, payment is usually offered as part of an advertising package, which usually includes all media, with exclusive world rights for all time.

The usage fee or day rate will also depend on your reputation. Those starting out will invariably be offered less than an established photographer.

No-one wants to lose a sale or commission, so it pays to be flexible but commercial reuse of work should be paid for. Some magazines offer 100% of the original fee, some pay as little as 10% for reuse. Some will want world exclusive rights in perpetuity, which allows them to use it forever and wherever they want. Better is to negotiate a fee for a very specific and time-limited licence. There should be a payment for every additional right the client wants.

Photographers need to agree a clear limit to the rights licensed. However, if you are too adamant about licences and rates of pay, you may well alienate a client and find you are never used again. While not being aggressive, do ask if there is a fee for reuse, for say, foreign editions or web use or for reuse after a time period of say, six months or a year. You need to ascertain whether you can syndicate the pictures after any agreed time limit or put the photos with a stock library for resale.

If the rates offered are so low that you will not really make anything, be prepared to exercise your only other option–to walk away. Photographers need to strike a deal that is fair to both the client and to you. This often comes from experience but you also need a clear understanding of the markets for photographs.

It is a sad fact that there are now many photographers only too willing to work for very low fees (or even for free) in return for getting their work published. Being published may get your work and name known which can lead onto greater things but if every photographer agrees to work for next to nothing, clients will think this is the norm. These photographers do themselves and the industry no favours in the long term.

Press and Editorial Photo Syndication

The press in the UK usually want UK exclusive rights, although newspapers and many magazines invariably want syndication rights to articles and photographs, so they handle the resale of your pictures and take a percentage of the sale price. Syndication departments may be in a better position than you to resell, so it could be worthwhile, so long as you are getting your fair share of the sale price. This is especially true of news press work, which is time-sensitive.

You should agree what rights and syndication rights are being sold before submitting final high resolution pictures. Another option would be to use a press agency.

How to Charge

Photographers working on commission charge by time, typically by the day. The day rate includes an initial license for reproducing the work. A half day should not be half your day rate but at least 60% of it. Half day shoots need just as much pre and post production work as full day shoots.

Some photographers charge a digital surcharge on top of their commission fee, which helps offset any post-production digital work, such as retouching (something clients increasingly demand from photographers, rather than commissioning a specialist retoucher).

Although day rates vary enormously, they must be enough to pay you a decent salary. Take into account that a day rate does not include your time preparing for the shoot, the days you spent talking to the client, days on post production, overheads, capital investment, delivery etc. Although digital photography and the internet has made post production and delivery easier, it still takes time. It is unlikely you can realistically get more than a couple of days per week photographing on commission, unless you have an army of assistants. Allowing for two weeks a year vacation and working 50 weeks a year, you might try this sobering calculation:

> *commission day rate average x two days a week x 50 weeks a year = projected annual income.*

Add up your annual overheads (the expenses you cannot reclaim from clients): rent, rates, utilities, staff, marketing material, phone, pension plans, etc and take away from that annual income figure. Then deduct the tax you have to pay. While you can claim most business expenses against tax, it will at least give you an idea of what your actual income might be for 50 weeks.

Of course, this doesn't include the huge capital amount you have had to pay for camera gear, software, computers etc.

The NUJ provides a calculator for photographers to work out their own figures.: *www.nuj.org.uk* or see *www.londonfreelancer.org*

Negotiating Rates

Commissioning editors and art directors may ask your day rate or half day rate so you need some idea of your rates for a particular client (which may differ for other clients) before you meet. They may try and beat you down so it is can be worth pricing your day rate at least 10% higher than you are willing to work for, to allow yourself some negotiating leeway to drop your price by 10%.

Many who commission photography will already have rates in mind. They know their own budgets and must work within them. Some, being in the business of making money for their own organisations, offer the lowest they think they can get away with. This doesn't mean you have to totally accept their offer. You always ask (nicely) if they could increase it a bit as you very rarely work for that amount. If you don't ask, you don't get and there may be some leeway in the budget. You could also increase your fee by politely explaining that there will be expenses for travel, props, stylists, post-production etc., for which you will have to bill them.

However, some clients may ask you to photograph something for less, with the promise of more next time. It rarely happens. Once you have set your value, it is very difficult to ask for more next time. They may also say they can't pay but will give you a credit line. While occasionally useful for new/young photographers as a way of building their portfolio and 'brand', it is highly unprofessional. A six point byline run alongside the pictures isn't going to pay the rent. The buyer gets paid, their company makes money, and so should you. Don't sell yourself short.

There have been stories of picture editors asking

1. 'This should only take you an hour, so I will only pay an hourly rate.' Gently mention setting up time and studio rent if needed, travel time if on location, pre and post production time and costs.
2. 'While you are there, can you shoot X as part of the deal?' Ask if it is part of the same story. If it is a separate story, it should be a separate budget, although you could negotiate a lower fee as you going to the location anyway.
3. 'Can you drop into Liverpool on your way to Ludlow for a quick shot of Mrs Y?' You are driving from your home in Bath for a one day shoot. Get out a map, explain it is not realistic but that you would be happy to do another shoot another day.
4. 'I can only afford to commission a couple of pictures.' The commission will take all day, in travel, organisation and taking the shots, so they should pay the day rate.
5. 'I could always buy stock instead.' Yes, they can but they won't, unless they pay for it, get anything unique for their publication.

Newspapers, magazines and adverts rely on having unique images to keep their reputation high, which in return reflects in sales and income from ad revenue.

6. One photographer was offered a very small fee for a job. 'It will only take you an hour or two'. His reply was that it has taken three years at college and fifteen years' working to get to the level required, quite apart from the ten grand spent on camera gear. The picture editor was so surprised she increased the fee to a reasonable day rate.

Selling Stock Direct

If selling stock via a stock library or agency, the rights and price is largely out of your control. You will already have a contract and the stock library or agency will deal on your behalf.

If selling stock direct, perhaps to a newspaper or magazine, you need to know what rights (license) they want. Is it exclusive, to be used only by them at any time, anywhere? This should be a higher fee than, for example, buying single use, one time UK rights only for, say, a year in specified media. The latter ensures some exclusivity in the UK and may allow you to sell the work elsewhere. However, be aware that most print media also have a web presence, so your UK exclusive will automatically be worldwide if used on the web. Web rights and fees should be on top of those for print use, unless you have agreed otherwise. It may be you agree a year's license for use in specified media and territories, after which you can renegotiate a license.

Bids

Occasionally, clients will shortlist a few photographers for a job and ask them to bid. You need to work out a rate and then add a contingency fee (at least 10% as bad stuff happens). This rate should include your time, (how long you think the job will take, including post-production, any travel, phone calls, rental costs, equipment, studio, vehicles, etc), and costs of an assistant if used. The job may be problematic and take much longer than you thought but if it takes less, you will still be able to charge the bid rate.

It can be tempting to bid low, to get the job. However, research shows this is not always the best strategy. People tend to choose the mid-range or second cheapest over the cheapest: that dead cheap roofer, the lowest bid on a plumbing job, the cheapest wine on the menu—it is the same for photographers. If your bid is very low, way under that of other photographers, the perception may be that you are not as good. Set the bar too low and you'll be unable to raise prices later.

Of course, you won't know what others have bid. That is one reason to look at industry standards and talk to other photographers, to get some idea of what they would charge. It is said that if a client isn't complaining a little about your rates, you probably aren't charging enough.

Estimates

Estimates are different. Work out your costs for the job (your day rate or pro rata, equipment hire, travel costs, assistants etc), add in an estimate for post production costs. If the job is on location, add in an estimate for bad weather days (usually around half your half day or day rate for the job). However, if your estimate is accepted and the whole thing goes smoothly with no bad weather, and the post production costs are much less than you thought, the final bill you submit should be lower than your estimate. This will also win you brownie points with the client.

Chapter Sixteen

Your Legal Trading Entity

You can operate a photographic business in several ways

1. A sole trader
2. A private limited company (with one or more directors)
3. A private unlimited company
4. A Partnership (with one or more partners)
5. A limited liability partnership (LLP)

1. Sole Trader

The majority of photographers are sole traders, (freelance, self-employed, call it what you will but it is you working for yourself). Sole traders must register as such with Her Majesty's Customs and Revenue as soon as possible after they start trading. The latest you can register is by 5 October after the end of the tax year for which you need a tax return. The official tax year runs from 6 April one year to 5 April the next. Your own tax year may be different, depending on when you started as self-employed.

You can call your sole tradership business almost anything you want (so long as it doesn't step on the toes of an established business), and you will be known as 'Your Name T/A (Trading As) Name of Your Business'. For example: Joe Smith T/A Smith Studios.

Employment with Freelance

If you have a job, full or part-time, under which your employer deducts tax at source (under Pay As You Earn, PAYE) but you have other income from other sources, you will probably need to complete a Self-Assessment Tax Return.

2. Private limited companies

A private company must be registered (incorporated) at Companies House and must file its accounts annually with Companies House. The accounts must be audited. A private company must send an annual return to Companies House (you can do this online using its web-filing system)

Both private limited and unlimited companies must also have at least one member and at least one director.

Any profits are usually distributed to shareholders in the form of dividends, apart from profits retained in the business as working capital.

You must tell HM Revenue & Customs (HMRC) that your company exists and is liable to Corporation Tax. You must then pay any Corporation Tax that is due and submit a Company Tax Return to HMRC. Companies also need to comply with HMRC's requirements for PAYE for employers, VAT etc.

Forming a Company

Limited companies exist as an entity in their own right. This means the company's finances are separate from the personal finances of their owners.

A company may be limited by shares or limited by guarantee. A company is limited by shares if members' liability is limited to the amount, if any, unpaid on the shares held by them. A company is limited by guarantee if members' liability is limited to an amount the members agree to contribute to the company in the event of its being wound up. There are also private unlimited companies but as there is no limit on the liability of its members, there is no real advantage to those in business and are therefore rare.

The Bigger Picture

For a company limited by shares, shareholders are not responsible for the company's debts unless they have given guarantees—for example, to guarantee a bank loan if the company defaults.

Shareholders may, of course, lose the money they have invested in the company if it fails. Shareholders may be individuals or other companies but shares cannot be offered to the general public.

Tax and National Insurance for Company Directors

Becoming a director sounds exciting but it brings with it responsibilities, including being held responsible for ensuring that annual tax returns are submitted to Companies House and that any corporation tax is paid on time. Company directors are office holders of the company and therefore regarded as employed earners for the purposes of paying National Insurance contributions (NICs). As such, company directors must pay both Income Tax and Class 1 NICs on their directors' earnings.

However, while regular employees' Class 1 NICs are calculated on their monthly or weekly earnings separately, directors' NICs are calculated on earning on an annual cumulative basis.

3. Partnerships

There are three types of partnership:

1. 'ordinary' partnerships
2. limited partnerships
3. limited liability partnerships (LLPs)

All three types of partnership have the following features in common:

- ◆ two or more persons who become business partners and share the risks, costs and responsibilities of being in business
- ◆ a partner can be an individual or another business, for example, a limited company or another partnership
- ◆ each partner takes an equal share of the profits, unless the partnership agreement states otherwise

- income tax and Class 4 National Insurance contributions are deducted from each partner's share of the profits
- each partner must register as self-employed with HM Revenue & Customs (HMRC) and complete an annual self-assessment tax return
- a nominated partner must also send HMRC a partnership return
- partners raise money for the business out of their own assets and/or with loans
- the partners themselves usually manage the business, although they can delegate certain responsibilities to employees

There are also 'sleeping' partners who contribute money to the business but are not involved in the day-to-day running of the business.

The partnership must keep records showing business income and expenses

Partnership Agreements

It cannot be stressed enough how important it is to have a partnership agreement. Always draw up a written agreement between the partners, specifying who is responsible for what, what percentage of income each will get, what expenses they can claim, working hours, holidays, what happens if the partnership breaks up, etc. Do not rely on being in partnership without one, regardless of whether the other partners are family or best friends. Not having an agreement has ended many a friendship and caused multiple disputes, and can spell disaster for a business.

'Ordinary' Partnerships

An 'ordinary' partnership has no legal existence distinct from the partners themselves. If one of the partners resigns, dies or goes bankrupt, the partnership must be dissolved—although the business can still continue.

A partnership is the simplest way for two or more people to own and run a business together. Partners are jointly liable for any debts owed by the partnership and so are equally responsible for paying off the whole debt. Any creditors can claim a partner's personal assets to pay off any debts—even those debts caused by other partners.

If a partner leaves the partnership, the remaining partners may be liable for the entire debt of the partnership. In this sort of partnership, the partners do not enjoy any financial protection if the business fails.

Limited Partnerships

A limited partnership is made up of one or more general partners and one or more limited partners. General partners are jointly liable for any debts owed by the partnership and so are equally responsible for paying off the whole debt.

A limited partner's liability is limited to the amount of money they have invested in the business and to any personal guarantees they have given to raise finance.

Limited partnerships must register with Companies House but don't generally have to make an annual return or file accounts.

Limited Liability Partnerships (LLPs)

LLPs must have a minimum of two designated members (i.e. partners) and must register with Companies House, send Companies House an annual return and file accounts with Companies House

A partner's liability is limited to the amount of money they have invested in the business and to any personal guarantees they have given to raise finance. This means that partner members have some protection if the business runs into trouble.

Chapter Seventeen

The Inevitable: Tax, Nics and Vat

'In this world nothing can be said to be certain, except death and taxes.'

—Benjamin Franklin, 1789

If you are employed in a job, with an employer, you will have tax and National Insurance contributions (NICs) deducted at source (before you see a penny) through the Pay As You Earn (PAYE) system.

Many photographers, however, work for themselves, and whichever entity you choose (freelance, partnership or company) to operate to trade, you will have to pay tax, or at least account for what you have earned and spent, regardless of whether you have made a profit or a loss. You do this by completing a Self-Assessment Tax return each year. If you do not receive a self-assessment tax return form after registering, ring the tax office and ask for one. Telephone HMRC Self Assessment helpline on 0845 9000 444. From abroad, telephone 0044 161 931 9070. Lines are open Mon-Fri 8am to 8pm, Sat 8am to 4pm, or visit *www.hmrc.gov.uk*. The onus is on you: not receiving a SA form is no excuse.

You must fill in and return your tax form by 31 January every year and pay any tax due by the same date. Miss this deadline and you immediately get a fine, with further fines (called penalties) for every delay, underpayment or mistake. These penalties are due to increase substantially. You pay tax on your income (less legitimate business expenses) for the previous tax year and make a first payment on account (i.e. in advance) for the next tax year.

On 31st July, you pay a second instalment of tax on account for the current year. If you think your earnings will diminish, you can ask for the amount on account to be reduced.

Employment with Freelance

If you have a job, full or part-time, under which your employer deducts tax at source (under Pay As You Earn, PAYE) but you have other income from other sources, you will need to complete a Self-Assessment Tax Return.

Who needs to complete a tax return:

You usually have to complete a tax return if:

- you are self-employed or in a partnership
- you are a company director
- you receive income from savings and investments
- you receive income from property
- you receive annual trust or settlement income on which tax is still due
- you receive income from the estate of a deceased person on which tax is still due
- you receive income from overseas that is liable to UK tax
- you are employed and want to claim expenses or professional subscriptions of £2,500 or more (less than this you can just write to HMRC)

Self Assessment Help

There are a few exceptions, when you have income and don't need to declare it, but do take professional advice. An accountant can explain these and advise whether you need to file a tax return and what you need to declare or you can ask HMRC direct.

Capital Gains Tax

Capital Gains Tax is a complex subject but if you bought a rare print and sold it for a fortune, you may well have a CGT bill to pay. HMRC's website gives details and the annual amount of exemption, the amount of profit allowed on a sale before you pay CGT.

Freelancers often forget that although Capital Gains Tax is not payable on your main home, if you use a specific part or room in it for business, CGT may be payable when you sell. Use your spare bedroom as an office, convert your garage to a working studio, and you could find yourself paying CGT on that portion of your main home when you sell. Declaring you work all over the house–the dining room table, the kitchen, everywhere, will help.

As well as tax…there's

National Insurance Contributions

If you're self-employed you pay Class 2 and Class 4 National Insurance contributions.

Low earners may not have to pay all NICs.

From April 2011, Class 2 National Insurance contributions payments will become due on 31 January and 31 July, the same as a Self Assessment tax bill. You pay Class 2 National Insurance contributions either monthly or six monthly by Direct Debit. You pay Class 4 National Insurance contributions when you pay your Income Tax.

VAT

Value Added Tax is a tax set by Her Majesty's Revenue & Customs (HMRC) on business products and services. The current (2011) VAT rate is 20% on most goods and services. Some goods, like books and newspapers, are currently exempt from charging VAT. A few, like car seats for children, carry a reduced rate.

If your annual turnover exceeds £73,000 a year (2011), you must, by law, register for VAT. Your turnover is the sum of all the goods you've sold and services you've provided in a VATable group. The government usually changes the VAT threshold once a year, announced in the Budget. You should check your turnover regularly and see if it doesn't outstrip the current VAT threshold. If it does—you have to register for VAT. If your turnover (rather than profits) hasn't exceeded the threshold yet, but you think it will outstrip it in 30 days, you must register for VAT.

Once registered, you must also add VAT (currently at 20%) to your invoices and pay that amount to HMRC. However, by being Vat registered, you can reclaim the VAT you have been charged on most business equipment, such as new cameras, computers and software.

To make life a bit simpler for VAT registered photographers, you can register in your first year as a VAT registered business for what is known as a flat rate, currently 11%. Here you charge VAT at the 20% rate (except on some exempt items) but you pay HMRC the lower flat rate percentage of the value of your invoices.

This flat rate is often subject to annual change, so it is worth checking the HMRC website.

You can apply for voluntary VAT registration if your turnover is below the VAT threshold, which means you can then reclaim the VAT on anything you buy new for business. You can also use the 'cash accounting' scheme—you only pay the VAT to HMRC when you have been paid.

You have to submit a quarterly VAT return, (though you can apply to do so annually) and keep very accurate accounts. If you register for VAT, expect a VAT inspection at your home or studio within two years. Get it wrong and you may receive a nasty fine. You must keep all records of VAT for at least six years.

When you should—and shouldn't—register for VAT.
If your clients are VAT registered, you should be too as it won't make any difference to your prices for them. However, if you are VAT registered and sell to the general public or anyone who is not VAT registered, you then have to charge VAT, making your fees 20% more expensive.

VAT is a complex subject but there is a detailed explanation on HMRC's website: *www.hmrc.gov.uk*

Record Keeping

Whichever way you chose to trade, you must keep records, whether you are VAT registered or not. You must keep these records for a further five years after 31st January deadline of your tax return. Keep all receipts, copies of invoices (paper versions are a wise backup, although HMRC will accept computer records), bank statements, business loan statements, cash books, rent books, pay slips for employees, accounting books and, if applicable, copies of your VAT returns.

Ask your bank and/or building society/investment company for an annual interest statement for any savings accounts, if you are not automatically sent one, which states how much you have in savings and how much tax you have paid. You need all this information for your annual self-assessment tax return. You will also need it if HMRC decides to investigate you and to go back over previous years.

You can claim many of your business expenses against tax, as well as deducting a certain amount for depreciation, capital expenditure etc. HMRC's website has details of what you can, and cannot, claim.

Hiring a Book-Keeper

If you can't trust yourself to keep accurate records and accounts or to file your VAT return, if you are VAT registered, then you might consider hiring a freelance book-keeper. For most photographers, asking them to do your accounts once a month or even every quarter will be enough.

Book-keepers will not only make your tax return simpler but will ensure you can claim tax relief on everything possible. You can even claim tax relief on their fees. Book-keeper rates vary according to the complexity of the work but £50-£60 a quarter seems to be the going rate for self-employed clients with very simple accounts.

Hiring an Accountant

A good accountant should make sure you claim everything against tax that you can legally claim as a business expense. A good accountant can often save you more in tax than their fees. They will also complete your self-assessment form for you and deal direct with the Inland Revenue on your behalf. S/he will save you hours. A good accountant is worth every penny and again, you can offset their fees against tax.

Your accountant can co-ordinate with your book-keeper, if you have one. If not, an accountant will take your books or computer spread sheets or even shoe-boxes of bits of papers and draw up year-end accounts and complete your self-assessment form on time. Obviously, the more organised you are and the better your own book-keeping, the less time it will take your accountant and the less, one hopes, their fees.

Give all your previous tax year financial information to your accountant after 6th April each. Accountants get very busy in December and January, so don't leave it to the last moment. If you do and the accountant simply cannot do your self-assessment return in time for the 31st January deadline, it is your fault, not theirs. It is you who will be fined.

To Find an Accountant

The best recommendation for both book-keepers and accountants is word-of-mouth. Ask other photographers, family and friends. For simple accounts and self-assessment tax returns for the self-employed expect to pay £200-300 a year. Larger accountancy firms with big overheads will charge a lot more.

You should always get three quotes and a), meet to ensure you get on, b), that s/he understands your type of business and c), ask for references.

It is worth asking for a fixed fee quote, rather than an hourly rate or, as some accountants demand, a monthly retainer (unless it is a reasonable amount and there will not be another huge bill later). Remember to add in the 20% VAT they will charge. You can reclaim this if you too are VAT registered.

You can find book-keepers at:

The Institute of Certified Bookkeepers: www.bookkeepers.org.uk.

To find accountants:

The Association of Chartered Certified Accountants: www.acca.co.uk.

The Institute of Chartered Accountants: (www.icaew.com for England and Wales: www.icas.org.uk for Scotland and www.icai.ie for Northern Ireland).

Simple Accounts for a Freelance Photographer

The new tax year in the UK begins on the 6th April every year. Not everyone has a 5th April tax year end.

Create a simple spreadsheet on computer or use accounting software, such as Sage, Intuit or Pegasus. One popular with photographers is Light Blue, www.lightbluesoftware.com. Just ensure, whichever you chose, it is compatible with that of your accountant, if you have one. Your choice is also dictated by the complexity and size of your business.

You can create one spreadsheet for income and another for outgoings/expenses.

Expenses

For each expense, you need:

Column 1: The date of the expense

Column 2: Who you are paying

Column 3: How you are paying (cheque/card/cash)

Column 4,5,6,7 etc: Use column headings of postage, travel, rent, equipment, utilities, freelance staff, etc., and put the amount under the relevant column heading.

This means you can easily see and add up what you spent on say, rent.

(If you are VAT registered, put the amount less the VAT element in these columns).

Second to last column: put the VAT element in its own column).

Last column: Put the total. If you are VAT registered, put the amount plus VAT here.

While keeping a record of every expense is a good idea, not every expense is allowable against tax by HMRC. Check the HMRC website to see what, and what is not, allowable. Your accountant will also know and include in your accounts every expense you can legally claim against tax.

Spread sheet accounts for income

Column 1: the date of your invoice

Column 2: your invoice reference number (you could also put the client's name)

Column 3: the amount you have charged..(less Vat if you are Vat registered),

Column 4: any expenses you invoiced the client,

Column 5: the Vat if you charged it,

Column 6: the total of the invoice.

Column 7: date and amount paid.

Column 8. How you are paid (Cash/cheque/credit card/debit card/ BACs, Paypal etc)

If you are Vat registered, the date you are paid is important, if you use what is called the Cash Accounting Scheme (meaning you only pay HMRC the VAT once you have been paid).

You could also have a petty cash book, if you need small amounts of cash to buy, say, fresh flowers for props. This enables you to keep track of small expenses and act as a record for your tax return.

You can see a full guide to keeping records on www.businesslink.gov.uk

How to Check a Client is Solvent

Companies that are solvent and reliable often publish their annual accounts on their websites. You can check out potential UK clients if they are a limited company on *www.companieshouse.gov.uk*. You can, for a small fee, see its last annual return, to determine the financial health of the company. For a credit report, you can buy one through *www.ukdata.com*

For individual clients, it is much harder. An internet search may bring up their name and address, and forums may tell you facts about them. Also search sites like Facebook and LinkedIn and Twitter.

Invoices

Unless the publication or agency you sell to operates a self-billing system, you must send an invoice. This should be on your headed paper (or at least with your name, address, contact numbers). An invoice can also be sent by email.

1. Write the name and address of the person/company you are invoicing.
2. Write the date the invoice is prepared.
3. Write a brief description of the job and the date of the work.
4. Put the fee you are charging on the right-hand side.
5. Add any extras agreed for expenses, under the fee. (If you are billing expenses, you also need to send the client the receipts—you cannot use these expenses again to claim against your tax).
6. If you are VAT registered, it is a legal requirement to add VAT under this column and identify it as VAT, Put your VAT number on the invoice. You also need to put a 'tax point', a date when the services were supplied, which might differ from the invoice date.
7. Put the total on the right hand side of the invoice, either under-lined or in bold.
8. You should also write your terms (the time scale by which the invoice must be paid): For example TERMS: 14 DAYS.

You should also write that no licensing rights whatsoever in these photographs are granted until you have been paid.

If you do not agree on terms with a client, the law automatically sets a default of 30 days.

Sometimes, invoices carry a small discount if they are paid according to your terms and conditions or paid early. 3-5% off the total is usual.

You are entitled to charge interest if payment is late, although you are in danger of upsetting clients. Currently, this is 8% plus the Bank of England's reference rate (at the time of writing, 0.5%), so you could add 8.5% for late payment. You can also claim reasonable debt recovery costs. The amount of compensation varies in accordance with the size of the debt.

Overdue Payments

If you are not paid by the date of your terms, send a statement (exactly the same as the invoice, but write 'statement'). If you are still not paid, send another with large red letters; THIS IS OVERDUE. Only you can decide whether to add the Late Payment percentage.

If payment is still not forthcoming, phone the accounts department, asking when it will be paid. It is probably not a good idea, at this stage, to phone the person who commissioned you, unless it is a very small company. Keep phoning, and if there is still no payment, call the client direct and explain you are having trouble getting paid. If the client is suddenly unavailable every time you call, try getting someone else to call or change your name for the call—you may be put through.

If still no payment arrives, go to the office. HMRC does this for outstanding tax, so there is no reason you can't. Just keep it professional and calm, demand a cheque and bank it immediately, in the hope you beat them before they cancel it. You could also suggest that a post-dated cheque would be acceptable, even though the client has every intention of cancelling it before you can bank it. However, this usually acts as proof the debt is undisputed and so, if it is subsequently cancelled, you can initiate formal recovery proceedings.

If a statutory demand has been issued and the debt remains unpaid for 21 days, on the whole this is evidence that the debt is good and undisputed. A threat of liquidation is often enough to get paid. However, if the client really cannot pay, threatening liquidation probably won't achieve much, though it may push you to the front of the debt queue. If the client is just going through a cash flow crisis from which they are likely to recover, such an action will not endear you to them for future work,

It is one of the advantages of having a contract that is legally binding. If a client won't issue a contract or sign one, it is usually a warning sign.

Some photographers ask for a deposit as a commitment to the job, which they then deduct from the final invoice. Wedding photographers may ask for anything from 10-30%, which is non-refundable should the couple cancel the wedding. Portrait or product photographers may ask for 10-15% deposit, which again, is deducted from the final invoice.

On larger jobs, it may be worth arranging a payment schedule, so payments are made in stages. If a client falls behind in payments, you could refuse to go on with the job, although you risk upsetting the client. However, if you have already done some of the work, and the client has a deadline, it can be a last resort bargaining position. If it is a large job and/or overseas then many photographers will ask for 50-100% of expenses in advance.

If you have eventually been paid, and the client asks you to do more, think long and hard. Some jobs just aren't worth the hassle.

Chapter Eighteen

Insurance

Your camera gear is worth a lot of money and is a good prize for the thief, as it is easily sold on. However, camera equipment devalues very quickly and, depending on your gear, it may not ultimately be worth paying the insurance premium if the insurance policy will not replace with new camera models (as older models are taken off the market). You definitely need a 'new for old' policy. Of course, it is not just the cameras: filters, memory cards, batteries, lights, tripods, bags....it all adds up.

Insurance companies may argue that the stolen, lost or damaged replacement you want is better than the one lost or stolen. Argue back if the lost camera model is no longer available and the new version is the same price (or less) than you originally paid, or offer to pay the difference if it is a lot more.

Your home contents insurance may cover some gear in and even outside the home but there may well be clauses that limit the value of a single item or not cover it at all if it is used by professionals. It may not cover you outside the UK. You might be able to pay a bit extra and get higher valued items to be taken outside the home included on home insurance but find out if it covers you abroad.

Many general insurers will consider professional photographic gear but there are also firms that offer specialist insurances for photographers, listed in this chapter. Be aware that while your home contents insurance usually covers your computer, it may not if you use it in any way for business, even if it never leaves your home. Reading the small print in your home insurance policy is essential.

Keep all receipts in a safe place (along with a note of the serial numbers) of any cameras, lenses, laptops etc. You will need these receipts for your annual accounts anyway.

Checklist for insurance for photographers.

- Camera and gadget insurance should cover your gear for loss, theft and damage (including accidental damage, which may be separately listed)
- You want a policy that offers new for old (you don't want to have to search the web for the same camera second hand)..
- Make sure it covers other items too, like your bag, filters, batteries, memory cards, tripod etc.
- Insure your laptop and mobile phone and if you use them for business, tell the insurer.
- Check what the excess is, if there is one. It may be the insurer won't pay the first £100-150 of value. The higher the excess you agree to pay, usually the lower the premium.
- Check that it covers camera gear if taken from the boot of your car. One company has been criticised as it will not cover theft from cars where the boot can be accessed from inside the car, as with many hatchbacks.
- Check where in the world it covers you for loss or theft—you may have to pay more for worldwide cover,
- Check the exemptions—the contract may not cover your camera gear if you go mountain climbing or white water rafting. There are certain countries which may also carry a premium. Photographers invariably pay more for camera insurance (as well as personal/health insurance) in war zones.
- Travel insurance usually has an excess and a claim's limit up to a set amount for lost or stolen items, which may not be enough. You may need specialist insurance (see list). Your travel insurance may not cover camera gear in the UK. Home insurance may not cover your gear outside the home.

- Many insurance companies will not cover camera gear that is checked into the hold of an aircraft. Always try and carry your camera gear as hand luggage.
- You should state that you are professional—which may make the insurance pricier. Don't be tempted to lie—it will invariably make any claim invalid.
- Some insurers have time limits on the length of each trip abroad. If going abroad, ensure you are covered for long enough.
- Professional indemnity insurance—Specialist insurers for photographers should offer this as part of their service.
- Public liability insurance—similarly, insurance for accidental damage or causing harm to property or people is also vital.

Public Liability Insurance

If you accept any money, including expenses, for work, you really should have Public Liability cover. Public Liability, or PL as it is known, covers your liability for any accidental damage to a person or property while working. Photographers with studios and on location at other business premises, or at home if the public visits for work, need PL.

PL should also cover third party damage to property. Knock that Ming vase off a client's shelf and you are probably going to be liable. Someone trips over your tripod, breaks a leg and sues... a venue or client will want your insurance, not theirs, to pay. There may well be an excess to pay (the proportion of the claim you have to pay, while the insurance company pays the rest) for PL third party cover. Most venues, such as local authority, hotels, music venues etc., simply won't allow a photographer to work on their premises without it. Many demand PL cover of £5 million, although you can opt for £1m, £2m, £3m or £4m cover.

If you undertake work in airports, in the air, underwater or on the ground by the side of rails or track side at motor events then you will need the higher limit and expect to pay more as insurers regard these activities as a greater risk.

A cautionary tale

In our blame culture, it is increasingly common for people to try and sue for every accident caused by something or someone else. While it may seem like a waste of money for the premiums, it really isn't. In the USA, event and police photographers spend much of their time photographing and videoing public events, which they keep as evidence, in case anyone fakes a fall and sues.

A UK photographer was doing some work for a Local Authority. As he was taking a shot, he stepped back and knocked over a woman behind him. She fell, hit her head on the pavement which left her severely brain damaged and in need of 24 hour care. The family sued the photographer and won £3 million in damages. Luckily, he had Public Liability cover of £5 million.

Professional Indemnity Insurance

Professional Indemnity Insurance (PI) covers your liability for failing to produce work to a professional standard. Claims can occur where a client or other person suffers financial loss as a result of alleged errors or omissions on your part. If the client is not satisfied with your work and tries to sue you for financial loss (which might occur if you do, for example, a product shot that needs re-shooting, and therefore delays the product's launch), you will incur substantial legal costs.

PI cover is important for when you are paid to photograph one-off events like weddings, (though try and ensure the bride and groom are covered too, with wedding insurance). If your memory card fails, and you have no photographs to show, they could sue you.

If you have bought PI or PL cover, make sure the insurer puts in writing that they cover you for professional photographic work. Don't accept their word for it over the phone.

Employee Liability Insurance

If you are a limited company with two or more working directors then you must, by law, have employee liability insurance, under the Employers Liability (Compulsory Insurance) Act 1969. It is also usual to have for Employers Liability if you have work experience students or volunteers assisting you, even if there is no payment.

Business Interruption

This type of insurance is popular for shops, galleries and studios. If your studio burns down or floods, you may have to hire another place to work (incurring costs) or stop working (loss of income) until your premises are back up and running.

Business Interruption insurance helps with costs towards you continuing in business, while Business Money insurance can help with cashflow in the case of disaster.

Keyman Insurance

You can insure yourself, a partner or key personnel in your business, with keyman insurance. This helps cover the costs of finding extra staff to replace the work done by a key person, should they fall ill or die. However, it can be very expensive.

Commercial Premises Insurance

Most insurers also offer commercial premises insurers, but do shop around as premiums vary greatly. You will need it if you have a studio—buildings insurance will be demanded by your mortgage company and landlord. Most commercial premises are let on commercial leases, which demand you have insurance.

If you rent an equipped studio by the hour or day, check the person or company renting it to you has both buildings and contents insurance and whether your own gear is covered by their insurance or if you need your own.

Specialist Insurers for Photographers and Their Gear

Aaduki Insurance: www.aaduki.com

AUA Insurance: www.aua-insurance.com

Gadget Cover: www.gadget-cover.com

Glover & Howe: www.gloverhowe.com

InFocus Photography Insurance: www.infocusinsurance.co.uk

Insurance4cameras: www.insurance4cameras.co.uk

Towergate Camerasure: www.towergatecamerasure.co.uk

Chapter Nineteen

Funding—Grants, Bursaries and Competitions

$\mathcal{T}$here are many opportunities for photographers to win bursaries, grants and awards. Some have specific rules on age, location or citizenship; a few even specify that they are for women only. Depending on budgets that year, grants do come and go or change their application rules. There are also hundreds of photographic competitions in the UK alone, and thousands run worldwide. The list given here, therefore, is not definitive.

Bursaries and awards can mean the financial freedom to complete a project, to travel, to exhibit or to publish. Winning competitions means prizes, often very valuable ones, of camera gear and/or money and possible inclusion in an exhibition. Being a winner of a bursary, award or competition is not just a welcome boost to your ego: it raises your profile and there is a lot of evidence to suggest that it can lead to greater things.

Competitions

Not all competitions are equal: some are definitely more prestigious than others. Professional photographers may turn their noses up at entering competitions, although, of course, they are delighted if they win 'photographer of the year' in their field. Magazines, newspapers and advertising agencies that have used your work may enter your pictures in a 'X photographer of the year' as they too recognise the prestige of an award.

A competitions may be a one-off, run as a fund raising venture by a charity. Competitions for landscapes, portraits, wildlife, pets, travel etc., photography are run by TV programmes, newspapers, magazines, websites and companies all the time, sometimes annually, sometimes monthly or as a one-off.

It is debatable whether you should pay to enter a competition, although even the prestigious Taylor Wessing National Portrait Gallery portrait prize charges an entry fee.

Do be aware that a few photographic competitions on websites which charge for entry are simply money-making exercises. They take your entry fee and your prize is just featuring on their website, or nothing at all.

Main Awards, Bursaries, and Competitions

Awards like those from the Winston Churchill Memorial Trust are not just for photographers. They are travel awards, which photographers have won in the past.

> Association of Photographers (UK) Open awards: www.the-aop.com
>
> The Aaron Siskind Foundation: www.aaronsiskind.org
>
> The Association of Photographers Awards (USA): www.the-awards.com
>
> The Ansel Adams Research Fellowship (USA): www.creativephotography.org
>
> Alexandra Boulat Scholarship: www.tpw.it
>
> Alexia Foundation (USA): www.alexiafoundation.org
>
> Amnesty Media Awards: www.amnesty.org.uk
>
> Aperture Portfolio Prize: www.aperture.org
>
> Arcimboldo Award for Digital Creation (France): www.arcimboldo-award.com
>
> Bayeux-Calvados Awards: www.prixbayeux.org
>
> Blurb Photobooks awards: www.photographybooknow.blurb.com/awards
>
> Burn Magazine/Magnum Foundation: www.burnmagazine.org

Bristol Natural History Consortium and Nature Picture Library Bursary: www.bnhc.org.uk and www.naturepl.com

British Journal of Photography: www.bjp-online.com

Canon Female Photojournalism Award: www.canonafjaward.com

Carmignac Gestion Photojournalism Award: www.carmignac.ch

Center Project Award: www.visitorcenter.org

Deutsche Gesallschaft fur Photographie e.v. (Germany): www.geo-union.de

Emerging Photographer Busary: www.garage-studios.co.uk

Environmental Photographer of the Year: www.ciwem.org

Epson Art Photo Award: www.art-photo-award.com

Ernest Cole Award (South Africa): www.ernestcoleaward.org

European Fund for Investigative Journalism: www.journalismfund.eu

European Publishers Award for Photography: www.dewilewispub lishing.com

F Award: www.fff.ph

Federation of European Professional Photographers, Photographer of the Year: www.europeanphotographers.eu

Fifty Crows (USA): www.fiftycrows.org

Foam and Paul Huf Awards: www.foammagazine.nl

Focus for Humanity:www.focusforhumanity.org

Format Festival: www.formatfestival.com

Foto8: www.foto8.com

FotoVisua Grant: http://grant.fotovisura.com

Freedom to Create Prize: www.freedomtocreate.com

FujiFilm Distinction Awards: www.fujifilmdistinctions.co.uk and www.choosefilm.com

Fujifilm/PPLA Colour printer Awards: www.fujifilm.co.uk

Fund for Investigative Journalism (USA): www.fij.org

Guardian Travel Photographer of the Year: www.guardian.co.uk

Getty Images Grants: http://imagery.gettyimages.com

The Hasselblad Foundation (Sweden): www.hasselbladfoundation.org

Henri Cartier-Bresson Award: www.henricartierbresson.org

Hey Hot Shot: www.heyhotshot.com

Hillman Foundation: www.hillmanfoundation.org

The Howard Chapnick Grant (USA): www.smithfund.org

Humanity Photo Awards: www.china-fpa.org

Humble Arts Foundation USA: www.haf.org

IdeasTap Photographic Award: www.ideastap.com

Inge Morath Foundation: www.ingemorath.org

International Garden Photographer of the Year: www.igpoty.com

Jerwood Photography Awards: www.jerwood.org

John Kobal Book Award: www.johnkobal.org

Kraszna-Kraausz Foundation Grants: www.editor.net

Landscape Photographer of the Year: www.take-a-view.com

London Photographic Awards: www.london-photographic-awards.com

Lumix Award: www.lumixaward.com

The Maine Photographic Workshops (USA): www.theworkshops.com

Magenta Foundation: www.magentafoundation.org

Magnum Awards: www.magnumphotos.com and blog: http://blog. magnumphotos.com

Manuel Rivera-Ortiz Foundation for International Photography: www.mrofoundation.org

The National Geographic Grant: http://ngm.nationalgeographic.com

The National Media Museum: www.nationalmediamuseum.org

Nikon Discovery Awards: www.nikon.co.uk

Noorderlicht International Photo Festival: www.noorderlicht.com

Oskar Barnack Prize: www.leica-camera.us

Ian Parry Award for Photographers: www.ianparry.org

The Picture Editors' Award: www.pictureawards.net

Press Photographer of the Year www.theppy.com

Royal Photographic Society Bursaries: www.rps.org
(also administers, with the Guardian The Joan Wakelin Bursary.)

Rhubarb-Rhubarb Bursaries: www.rhubarb-rhubard.net

W. Eugene Smith Grant in Humanistic Photography: www.smith fund.org

Spider Awards: www.spiderawards.co.uk

Silver Eye Center for Photography Fellowship: www.silvereye.org

Site Gallery Commissions Programme: www.sitegallery.org

Sports Photographer of the Year: www.pressawards/org

SUN Awards: www.shotupnorth.co.uk

Taylor Wessing Photographic Portrait Prize: www.npg.org.uk

Terry O'Neill Award: www.oneillaward.com

The Observer Hodge Photographic Awards: www.observer.co.uk

The Photocrati Fund: www.photocrati.com

The Pierre and Alexandra Boulet Association: www.viiphoto.com

The Polaroid International Photo Awards: www.polaroid.com

The Pulitzer Center on Crisis Reporting: www.pulitzercenter.org

The Times Young Photographer of the Year: www.thetimes.co.uk

Travel Photographer of the Year: www.tpoty.com

Unicef Photo of the Year: www.unicef.de

Vice Magazine/CTRL.ALT.SHIFT competition: www.ctrlaltshift.co.uk

Visa pour l'Image Perpignan: www.visapourlimage.com

Veolia Environment Wildlife Photographer of the Year (with the Natural History Museum): www.nhm.ac.uk

Voies Off (France): www.voiesoff.com

War on Want Document Photographic Award (Student award) www.documentphotoaward.org

Young Fashion Photographer of the Year: www.clothesshowlive.com

www.documentphotoaward.org

Px3: www.px3.fr

Reportage : Festival of Documentary Photography (AU) www.
reportage.com.au

Renaissance Photography Prize: www.renaissancephotography.org

Winston Churchill Memorial Trust: www.wcmt.org.uk

Sony World Photography Awards: www.worldphotographyawards.org

Financing Projects By Crowd Funding

If you have a photographic project you want to get off the ground, and no
funds are available from grants or other sources, you might consider crowd
funding. Although most crowd funding is for social benefit, there are film
makers and other artists using it. Crowd funding allows you to fund your
project by inviting fundraising online.

Instead of the usual fund raising/grant systems, and asking one person,
organisation or company for large amounts of funding, you ask a lot of
people for small amounts. You can post a project proposal in one of the
crowd sourcing websites below (more are coming online all the time). This
can be in the form of a written proposal, press release or even a short video.
In return, people (who, thanks to the internet, can come from anywhere in
the world) may be rewarded with gifts such as a mounted print or series of
prints or a photo book which includes a credit, photo shoot etc.

You can attract crowd funding if you spread the word through social media
sites like Facebook and Twitter, short videos on YouTube, and professional
networks like LinkedIn. Refer and link to the crowd sourcing site you have
chosen. You could also create a blog about the project. Make it very clear
what you are planning to do and why and make it compelling. It helps if a
third party will benefit, such as raising awareness of a social issue through a
photography exhibition or book, selling prints to raise money for a charity
etc. You can also email everyone in your address book, although be aware
of the Data Protection Act on email marketing and it is wise to be selective,
to email groups in batches. Ensure if you do a round robin email that the
addresses are hidden from others, unless you want to upset a lot of clients
and give away all your contacts.

Set a realistic budget. Keep the total amount quite low (perhaps no more than £2000), so the target seems reachable to prospective funders. If you need a higher amount, consider splitting the project into different parts, for example, to do the shoot and cover the travel costs, and secondly to mount an exhibition or produce a book. Most funders will not donate money for your purely indulgent dream of a month photographing the Seychelles. If it has a social benefit, it is more likely to succeed.

Most crowd funding sites will not let you access any money pledged if the full amount you have asked for is not met within the deadline. If unsuccessful, all money will be returned to the people who have donated so far.

Look at all crowd sourcing sites before deciding which to use. Some are more successful in raising money for buying cows in Africa than for arts and photography projects. Most charge the person posting a project a percentage of the amount they want to raise, usually 4-5%, and a few may demand you have a US bank account, though that is likely to change as crowd sourcing grows. Most also charge for use of credit cards and/or PayPal donations from funders, usually between 3-5% or a small fee, such as 50 pence. Read the terms and conditions carefully as they all vary.

The main crowd sourcing sites are:

CrowdCube–www.crowdcube.com

Kickstarter–www.kickstarter.com Creative industries

IndieGoGo–www.indiegogo.com Creative industries

We Fund–UK based, www.wefund.co.uk

WeDidThis–UK based, www.wedidthis.org.uk

Sponsume–www.sponsume.com

Crowdfunder–UK based, www.crowdfunder.co.uk

Fans Next Door–French site, en.fansnextdoor.com

Pozible–UK based, www.pozible.co.uk

Inkubato–www.inkubato.com

Rocket Hub–www.rockethub.com

Fundbreak–Australian, www.fundbreak.com.au

Chapter Twenty

Students

*P*hotography is now one of the most popular degree courses in the UK but is also one of the few professions where you don't need a degree. Many successful photographers are self taught, both in photography and the business side of photography. Others start as assistants to successful photographers. Some are fortunate enough to find a mentor.

Many successful photographers have had other careers first. Doctors, dentists, accountants, civil servants…many have successfully switched to being professional photographers.

Books and courses can teach you how to shoot. What they cannot do is teach you how to think. The major benefit of any sort of degree/higher education is the intellectual thought processes you learn. To qualify as degree courses, they must all include a certain amount of written, academic work.

A photography course can open your mind, allow you to experiment and take risks (that doesn't mean going to war zones, but taking visual risks, pushing your creative boundaries). Photography is a huge area, covering all forms of photography, from photojournalism to stop-motion work. Whatever your field of interest, you have time to try it on a degree course.

Looking at forums, one big debate is whether photography degrees are worth it, given the level of student debt most leave with. There are other options for training, or you could even try and get a job sweeping the floor in a studio, learning as you go and working your way up.

However, for three years of immersing yourself in a subject, studying not only the masters but also learning techniques, experimenting, finding your style and niche, making contacts, meeting and learning from your peers and for general enjoyment, almost all photography students say it is worth it. That said, despite the proliferation of photography degree courses, their popularity means that getting a place has never been more competitive. Many photographers also feel that the profession has reached saturation point, with too many photographers chasing too little work. One forum had at least a dozen photographers saying they wished they'd become doctors/accountants/lawyers instead.

Applying for a Degree or Foundation Degree Course in Photography

There are hundreds of UK courses in photography that offer degrees (a BA, or sometimes a BSc) and the vast majority are listed on the University and College Admissions Service, *www.ucas.com*, through which you also apply. Some universities/art colleges run photographic courses in specialist areas, such as photojournalism, fashion, even forensic. Some offer combined degrees with other subjects, both related and unrelated. Via the UCAS website, you can link to the website of each university/college and within that to details of its photography courses. Each university/college will also publish a printed version of its annual prospectus.

It can help with an application for a degree course if you have already studied photography or something related at A level or BTEC but it is not essential. If your school/college does not offer an appropriate course, consider doing a private one, even if only for a few days or at least join a camera club or a photography meet-up group. You can then mention it in your personal statement, a compulsory element of university applications. 'My school does not offer any photographic course, so I joined X camera club and took a short course with Y, as I felt I might otherwise be disadvantaged.'

Each course on each university's website will tell you how many educational points you need to apply: these are determined by adding up from your secondary educational exams results. The UCAS site tells you what each qualification, at each grade, is worth (click Students, then Tariff). Some universities/art colleges will filter applications by points first, before they even consider the personal statement every application must make or before inviting them to an interview.

If you don't have the right amount of points, don't despair. Most universities' art-based courses prefer to see a portfolio and meet you rather than base their decisions on academic achievements alone. Almost every university has what is called a 'widening participation' scheme, meaning they will consider students who do not have the usual academic background or qualifications. They will also consider mature students, often regardless of academic qualifications.

There are also Foundation Degrees in photography, two year courses (or part-time over a longer period) that can, if you want, lead onto a full degree. Foundation Degree courses are meant to be more practical and vocational. Some Foundation Degrees, such as the one at Westminster University, are not listed on the UCAS site and you have to apply direct to them. The universities/art colleges which run them can be found by an internet search. It also means you can apply for them as well as your five choices of degree courses allowed via UCAS.

Personal Statements

Whichever higher educational photographic degree or foundation degree course you apply for, you will need a personal statement. For applications through UCAS, the form only allows you up to 4000 characters (including spaces) or 47 lines for your personal statement. It could be the most important document you ever write, so take time to plan it. Look at the UCAS advice, ask teachers, and get family and friends to read and proof read it (don't rely on a spell-check). Some application forms for Foundation Degrees don't specify if you need a personal statement, but attach one anyway.

There are some personal statement examples for photography degree applications on the web (*www.studential.com* for example), but while useful as guidelines, don't plagiarise. Tutors will go mad if they read once more that 'there are X countries and X languages in the world … photography is an international way of communicating without language: it crosses boarders and cultures' etc... Don't lecture tutors on their own subject.

Include a line or two saying why you want to study photography at degree level. You need to convince the reader that you have the personal qualities, dedication and interests to study at university. Add achievements (including recent non-photographic ones) and what you learnt from them. Perhaps mention how much you liked X's photographs at the Y exhibition and why. Explain the latest photographic project you are working on, mention influences of style, state how you want to experiment with X, learn studio lighting to achieve Y. Tutors want to see evidence of a bit of thought, some get up and go, that you are open to new ideas, want to experiment and are willing to learn.

Personal Statement Tips

- Plan an outline.
- Type it as a document first, not on the UCAS form. You can then copy and paste on the UCAS site when you are happy. Check it again on the UCAS form, as different software programmes might change the format for things like quotation marks.
- Keep copies at each stage of writing your statement on disc, USB, email, DropBox etc.
- Try and make each sentence flow into the next. Similarly, try and relate the last line of one paragraph to the first of the next.
- Do write a personal statement about you, not a treatise on photography.
- State why you want to study photography at degree level. For example, you might state you want time to experiment, try different fields of photography and learn how past masters worked.
- Discuss it with your tutors and family, and get them to proof read it several times—every time you make an alteration.
- Only include things you are able to talk about at your interview.
- Write a little about hobbies and interests and try and relate them to photography. For instance: 'I am interested in wildlife and recently spent a week camping in the local woods, photographing animal

behaviour …' or 'I entered the X bike race last year and this year I am photographing all stages of the race for the organisers and to submit to Y publication.'

- Mention any recent positions of responsibility you have held and what skills you learnt, such as leadership, working without supervision etc. Don't include those from before GCSEs.
- Don't waste space and list your academic achievements—these are listed elsewhere on your application form. You can refer to one or more, for example, 'On X project for A level art, I used photography to…'
- Mention books, for example, 'Reading Susan Sontag's book on photography helped me understand how…'
- Mention photography exhibitions you have been to recently, what you liked and why.
- Mention a couple of successful photographers you admire, and why.
- UCAS has software that can spot plagiarism, which can end up with your application being disqualified.
- Don't write a statement addressing or naming one university only, unless you have made it your only choice.
- Don't write your statement as a letter (ie Dear Sir or Madam) or say 'Thank you for reading this'.
- If you are not sure where your degree will lead, and don't yet know which area of photography you want to go into after university, don't make anything up. If you are dead set on being a sports photography, mention it.
- Don't lie, exaggerate or boast. Sound confident, not arrogant. Say what you mean, without flowery language or long words you wouldn't normally use.

As a rough guide, 60% of your statement should be about why you want to do this course, and why at degree level; 30% on your experience and activities related directly to photography and 10% on unrelated hobbies and activities.

At the end of the statement, you could sum up why the university should take you and what an offer would mean to you.

You do not have to use every word allowed by UCAS. Be concise, use correct spelling and grammar, read through it to ensure it flows, and proof read it several times. Ask as many people as you can to read it, give you feedback and proof read it.

Interviews

If invited for interview, you should also be able to talk about your work and your statement and able to answer questions such as: Why do you want to study photography? Why here? Who is your favourite photographer and why? What photographic projects are you working on at the moment? What photographic exhibitions have you seen recently? What photography books are you reading? Do you prefer digital or film? Which is your favourite photo in your portfolio and why?

The interviewers are not trying to catch you out nor are there perfect answers. They want to hear you talk so they can get to know you. Tutors, invariably excellent photographers themselves, can spot talent—or rather, potential talent—and if they like the work and you, your enthusiasm and dedication, they may well offer you a place. Interviewers know you are nervous and will try and put you at ease. You may be interviewed alone, by one or two tutors, or in a group.

Be enthusiastic but not gushing, don't go on about how you have always loved photography since before you could talk (you didn't), don't say how good you are, and if they ask you why this university course, an answer like 'It has got a great reputation and industry contacts', or 'I really liked the work I saw at your last degree show' will help. You should research and have prior knowledge of the course as well as of the university.

Asked what field of photography you want to go into, it is quite alright to say you don't know yet—just use it as a positive for wanting to get onto the course and spend three years' experimenting and trying different sorts of photography.

If you are lucky enough to get several interviews, be enthusiastic about each. Universities are no longer told your order of choice through UCAS but you may well only get an offer from your second or even fifth preference.

Student Portfolios

You will also need a portfolio to show if invited for interview. Your portfolio should include 20–30 prints of your best photos. If you are not happy with work for A level/BTEC projects, set and shoot your own. There are plenty of project books available and ten project ideas are given here to get you started.

Offer to be the photographer on your school newspaper, website or year-book, Start a blog on photography. Enter local (or national if a photo is good enough) competitions. Get work experience, even sweeping the floor of a studio. It all shows a determination that will help make your application stand out over others.

For your portfolio, A4 prints are large enough. Mount prints on one side of card only and ensure they are evenly mounted, clean and tidy. First impressions count.

While some photographers now use an iPad to show their work, be aware that you may have to leave your work with tutors to look at when you are not present and most tutors will not want responsibility for your iPad. Most will want a traditional portfolio. Tutors will not want to look at work on your laptop, discs or USBs, but some ask you to bring a copy of your work on disc to leave with them. Some may ask you to make a few submissions online as the first step. Others may ask you to write something on a certain photograph or photographer. A few may even ask you to photograph and submit work to their brief.

If the course's website or your invitation to an interview says it wants to see some black and white film prints, beg or borrow a film camera, though you can pick them up for a song in charity shops and on eBay. Tutors don't expect you to have your own darkroom or even to know how to develop and print but it's another plus point if you can. Your local camera club or community/charity/private course photography centres may be able to help. If you can't get access to a darkroom and/or don't know how to print, an ad on a local/photography forum asking for help may work. Failing that, you need a professional studio, though it gets expensive.

Ask photography tutors what they want to see and they will usually say 'surprise me'. They all like portfolios with some sense of structure, rather

The Bigger Picture

than random shots: a portfolio that has cohesion, where one photo links, even tenuously, to the next. Make sure the first photograph wows them but that they are just as wowed by what comes after. They can always tell a portfolio that has been padded out. Remember, less is more, so 20 great shots is better than 40 okay shots.

It is almost easier to say what they do not want. One photography tutor, at an open day of a leading university, said that they did not want a portfolio that shouts: 'This is my project on shadows, this is my project on textures.' Nor do they want copycat styles, shots of lines of car lights at night, shots of long avenues of trees at sunset. Be inventive, use photography project books to come up with a series of photographs.

Pace your portfolio, both in photo size and subject but so that each photograph has some relationship to the one before it. If you are displaying your work on boards, use one side only. Lay out prints out on a table and spend time deciding your strongest shots and how they relate to the photo before and after it.

Many course interviewers ask for a sketch book too. This doesn't mean drawings or your sketchbook from A level art. It means contact prints, tear sheets of photographs you like, copies of interesting articles, some of your own writing on photography, rough prints marked for cropping, before and after blow-ups of sections of your photos. Tutors do not expect you to spend a fortune on this, so desktop prints, even on non-photographic paper, are fine for a sketchbook. If you have had worked published, put in tear sheets. If the credit line is very small, write a heading that makes it clear it is your work. This could also go at the back of your portfolio.

Open Days and Degree Shows

Go to as many open days as you can. You need to book for some open days. Also visit degree shows. Details of open days and degree shows are on the websites each university/college.

Apart from visiting your local university/art college degree show, travelling around the country is both expensive and impractical. A trip to London may be more cost-effective. Each year, in June and July, art colleges and universities from across the country come to London and show degree work at FreeRange held at the Truman Brewery in East London, *www.free-range.org.uk*. The website has a calendar of the degree shows, each course showing for a week. It means that not all photographer degree shows will be on at the same time, so pick the week where most of your preferred colleges are showing. You also have to make your UCAS course choice earlier in the year. Think ahead, and if you can, visit the year before you apply. Not every London photography degree course participates as they have shows at their own premises—time your visit well, and you may be able to visit them as well.

What the Prospectus Won't Tell You.

Some universities will only accept people onto its arts degree courses or foundation degree courses who have done a foundation course first, a one year general arts course. It is rumoured that foundation courses (not the same thing as two-year Foundation Degrees) are to be phased out.

Why You Need to Know About Compact Agreements

At present, some specialist art and design colleges/universities have a 'compact agreement'. A compact agreement means they are almost obliged to accept anyone from their own foundation course who applies to their degree courses. This is never mentioned in any prospectus.

One reason it is not mentioned is that they want as many people as possible to apply to their degree courses, as application numbers boost the kudos of the course and ensures it will continue (the Rector won't close a course that had 800 applicants).

If there is a compact agreement with its foundation courses, and the college has, for example, 40 places on the photography degree course and 40 people from its own foundation course apply, their course is full before you have even had an interview (if you get that far). At open days, ask if they require you to have done a foundation course before you apply. Ask if they give preference to those who have done its own foundation course and whether

The Bigger Picture

they have a compact agreement in place. Will they have places left to offer, if they first take people from its own foundation course?

If they do say a foundation course is usually essential, it could be worth considering applying to one. If they admit they have a compact agreement in place and you really want to go to that college for photography, it could be worth applying to its own foundation course first. Applying for its degree course without doing so could be wasting one of your five UCAS choices.

Universities also encourage students from outside the European Union–universities can charge more for these overseas students. Ask how many places are available in total on the course, what percentage of students they take from the UK and if they have a maximum intake of overseas students.

What is a foundation course?

A foundation course run by art colleges and the arts faculties of many universities is different from a Foundation Degree. It is a one-year further (rather than higher) education course in art and design. You get to do a bit of everything, from drawing and painting, sculpture, silk screen printing, etc. It is intended as a course to help you decide whether you want to go into graphics or typography, fashion or photography, for example. You will still need a good portfolio to get onto one of these courses, and they will want to see evidence of drawing, graphics etc in addition to photography.

Don't expect foundation courses to concentrate solely on photography. Most offer limited photography teaching, although you can use it in projects.

Some art colleges will only consider students for its degree courses who have completed a foundation course.

Other Courses

Many local authority colleges offer low-cost part-time or evening classes in photography for different levels, from beginners through to advanced. Always go for a level that will push you, without feeling you are out of your depth. You may also want to extend your knowledge in related fields, perhaps with a course on Adobe Creative Suite—colleges offer all sorts of courses useful to the photographer. You can find them on *www.hotcourses.com*.

Many universities and art colleges offer other photographic courses, at the weekend, summer holidays etc., as well as ABC Diploma courses (a formal qualification but not as high as a degree).

The National Council for Training Journalists (*www.nctj.org.uk*) offers accredited courses, although there are rumours they are to cut some courses, due to lack of funding. Not that they are free but they will cost less than three years at university. Some press agencies, such as The Press Association (*www.pressassociation.com*) also offer photography training courses.

The main photographic associations, listed below, also offer training and workshops. Some may offer financial assistance to attend a training course.

> The Association of Photographers: www.the-aop.org.uk
>
> The Royal Photographic Society: www.rps.org
>
> The British Institute of Professional Photographers: www.bipp.com
>
> The British Press Photographers' Association: www.thebppa.com
>
> Bureau of Freelance Photographers: www.thebfp.com
>
> Chartered Institute of Journalists: www.cioj.co.uk
>
> Guild of Photographers: www.photoguild.co.uk
>
> Master Photographers Association: www.thempa.com
>
> National Union of Journalists: www.nuj.org.uk
>
> Society of Wedding & Portrait Photographers: www.swpp.co.uk

Magnum, the consortium of the world's top photojournalists, offers bursaries for young people to attend its seminars and workshops: *www.ideastap. com*. There are also respected City and Guilds courses run throughout the UK: www.city-and-guilds.co.uk

Hundreds, if not thousands, of courses are also run by commercial companies or by not-for-profit organisations. These are full time, part time and online. Attending one may not give you a formal qualification but it will help you build your knowledge and portfolio. It can also help if mentioned in a personal statement, if you want to get onto a degree course. Many such courses are listed on *www.photographers.co.uk*, on other photography websites and are advertised in photography magazines. Some photographers also offer group or one-to-one tuition. They advertise on sites like *www.ephotozine.com*, Gumtree, Craigslist, Meet-up group sites, Facebook and local forums. Discount sites like GroupOn occasional runs offers for photography courses.

Residential Courses

There are also residential courses and workshops in the UK and overseas. A few offer bursaries, usually for under 25s. See Grants, Bursaries and Awards. Some companies offer photographic holidays, which might be a way of combining learning, building your portfolio and having a good time.

Search the web for 'training for photographers' and over 57 million results come back. Restrict it to the UK, you still get a staggering eight million plus results. How do you choose?

1. Get recommendations for courses from local forums and other photographers.
2. Location—can you easily get to the classes?
3. Are classes at times you can attend? You won't get a refund for not showing up.
4. Cost? Is the course good value—ask people who have been on the courses for their feedback via the course site and on local/photographic forums. Look at the quality of work produced (the course's site should show you examples).
5. Is the level of teaching high enough? You do not want a class that concentrates on how to use a compact camera but nor do you want a class that assumes too much and is way beyond your capabilities. You want a class that stretches you and teaches you something new.
6. Is it all class/studio based, or do you get out and about with a tutor?
7. If you want to learn studio and/or darkroom, what facilities do they have? How much time will each student get to use the studio/ darkroom?

8. Who is the tutor, what have they done, what is their work like?
9. How many people are on the course? Too many, and you won't get the tuition you want. What feedback do you receive and from whom?
10. What happens at the end of the course? Is there a certificate? Is there an exhibition?

For photography work experience and internships and student jobs, see *www.arts.ac.uk*, (London bias), *www.photoassist.co.uk* and local forums (see **Work**).

Ten Projects to Get You Started

The Royal Photographic Society has a learning centre on its website that is worth a visit (*www.rps.org*) and many other websites and competitions give photographic projects that may appeal. It really is worth doing as many projects as you can outside an A level or BTEC syllabus, as although no two students will interpret the exam projects in quite the same way, tutors will know that that year's set project was X, and will see hundreds of similar photos. You may think your interpretation is unique but it probably won't be.

1. Pick a word such as tenderness, friendship, love, hate, passion, decay, freedom etc., and interpret it through a series of photographs.
2. Chose one colour. Photograph everything that features, however obscurely, your chosen colour.
3. Pick one shape: Spiral, square, circle or triangle and photograph as many examples as you can see in the environment and architecture when out and about and at home. You could also use capital letters as shapes, A to Z, concentrating on one letter or do the whole alphabet.
4. Take a series of self-portraits, use reflections, textures, through windows, net curtains—be more imaginative than a formal portrait.
5. Photograph a series of silhouettes
6. Shoot a series of reflections seen in cars (in the windows, bumper, mirrors etc). Keep yourself out of the photograph.

7. Patterns in nature: Cut fruit and vegetables in half and photograph the cross-sections, or photograph patterns on leaves, in shell fish, landscapes etc

8. Take a photo essay on one subject: it could be night workers, lunchtime, British at play, my sibling, my neighbours and/or neighbourhood, the view from your window at different times of day.

9. Photograph found objects: as you walk around you will see all sorts of things discarded in the street.

10. People—photographed from the back or concentrate on just their eyes or feet or hands.

Chapter Twenty-One

Travel and the Photographer

*P*hotographers and travel usually go together like a horse and carriage. With the exception of studio based work, most photographers will have to travel and most are only too happy to do so.

It is obviously important to research the cultural requirements of the country you intend to visit before you go, (especially outside the so-called westernised countries). You should have the appropriate clothing, (female photographers in particular, should be aware of dress codes and whether they need to cover their heads/arms etc.).

You should learn even a few basic words to know how to meet and greet and explain what you are doing and for what. Always carry with you any letters of commissions you may have, although some photographers find that they get the job done better, with less hassle by officials, if they declare they are just tourists. Some journalists and photographers who travel a lot off the beaten track or to 'difficult' countries state in their passports that they are teachers or gardeners or in some other less contentious profession.

While there are excellent guidebooks to most destinations and most countries have their own tourist websites, it is worth checking the travel advice on The Foreign & Commonwealth Office (FCO) website, *www.fco.gov.uk*. It gives all the official details, such as VISA requirements, you need for each country, as well as advice on where travel is not recommended. If going off the beaten track, do register with its LOCATE register. It's free and can be invaluable for emergency contacts and finding you. The site also has details of the British Consulates around the world and when and how they will–and won't–help you.

In some countries (and indeed in some communities in the UK), people still believe that photography may take away their soul and object to you pointing a camera at them. Others may just not want their photograph taken, or demand money for posing.

Find out cultural norms, differences and country laws before you so much as lift your camera.

Do some research on cultural differences, body language and gestures: thumbs up in Saudi Arabia, for example, is as bad as giving someone the two fingers in the UK. A nod in Turkey and Bulgaria means no, while a shake of the head means yes. Eating with your left hand is considered offensive in some countries, while holding hands with your girlfriend in the street will be considered an outrage in others. In some countries it can be forbidden, or certainly frowned upon, to photograph women. A little knowledge and some language, even please, thank you, yes and no, gets you a long way. A smile, of course, is international.

Some photographers travelling off the beaten track will take along photos of their own family and postcards of their home town/country. These help break down barriers and postcards make good presents for children.

Your Own Safety

Photographers are particularly vulnerable when travelling. Your gear is expensive and you have to show it to use it. While your smart camera bag may be great, it shouts that it is full of cameras. Seasoned photographers often have tatty old bags and cover the logos with cheap badges.

It is wise to carry your passport and some money in an inner zipped pocket, bumbag and/or money belt. In most countries other than the UK, you have to carry an ID card or passport at all times. Put your mobile where it can be easily reached, keep it well charged and know the emergency services numbers of the country you are visiting. Keep other valuables in your hotel room safe, if it has one, or the hotel's own safe (and get a receipt).

A photographer's vest with lots of pockets is a good idea when travelling, worn under another jacket so it is not so visible. Less expensive than a photographer's vest is a fisherman's vest, available on eBay and other sites for under £10.

If you want to travel off the beaten track, a recommended local guide/driver is not only good security but will get you to places you might not otherwise see. Ask at the local tourist board, Chamber of Commerce or even the British Embassy or British Consulate. The concierge of a good hotel may also be able to help. There are numerous sites to find travel companions and guides, including:

www.lonelyplanet.com (Thorn Tree forum)

www.craigslist.com

www.rentalocalfriend.com

www.globetrooper.com

www.tripbod.com

www.bootnall.com

www.realtravel.com

www.tripmates.com

www.wanderlust.co.uk.

If you want to meet up with another photographer, most countries have their own photographic societies, associations and camera clubs. Try an internet search for photographic association/society with the name of the country you are visiting. You could also try *www.smugmug.com, www.meetup.com, www.travellerspoint.com, www.flickr.com, www.facebook.com,* and *www. lightstalkers.org,* described as Facebook for professional photographers.

You could also try searching the web for 'photographer' and the place you are visiting and make contact direct with other photographers. Many photography sites have membership lists of people in different countries, so it could be worth signing up (usually free) and seeing if there is a photographer where you want to go.

Most photographers are generous and like meeting other photographers. They might offer to act as a guide or recommend someone who would. Just make sure it is not a one-way street—give something back, whether offering advice, offering to host them in the UK, or to pay them. Sending a set of prints to him/her, whether a driver, guide or another photographer, is also a good idea—you never know when you might need them again. Some photographers now produce a photobook to send as a thank you.

Travellers on a tight budget can find spare rooms and sofas on:

    www.couchsurfing.com

    www.9flats.com

    www.istopover.com

    www.crashpadder.com

    www.wimdu.co.uk

    www.airbnb.com

There are also hostels worldwide—sites like *www.hostelbookers.com* and *www.youth-hostels.co.uk* give list of hostels, cheap hotels and apartments.

Another option is to search one of the traveller's forums or join, for a fee, a homeswap site. You could also do voluntary work or even crew, if you can sail.

    www.lonelyplanet.com

    www.intervac.co.uk

    www.homeexchange.com

    www.guardianhomeexchange.co.uk.

    www.vso.org.uk

    www.muchbetteradventure.com

    www.workaway.info

    www.wwoof.org

    www.crewseekers.net

www.wanderlust.co.uk also has ideas for cheap travel and gives website contacts. Cheap flights can be searched on sites like *www.kayak.co.uk, www.flycheapo.com, www.skyscanner.net* and *www.hipmunk.com.*

Some charities are also looking for photographers to cover their projects, often overseas. They may pay, or at least pay for flight and board and keep in return for use of the photographs. Try *www.charityjobs.co.uk* and *www.thirdsector.co.uk*.

Some charities charge you for a trip and ask you to raise money on their behalf by getting sponsors.

1. Keep with you, and separate from your passport, a copy of your passport, ticket, hotel bookings, insurance, any important medical information and VISA. Scan second copies and email them to yourself and to your next of kin. You could also store them with a file hosting service like Dropbox, but ensure your next of kin has access.
2. Always carry your digital storage cards on your person, not in your camera bag.
3. Make sure you have the right clothing for the climatic and other conditions of the area you are going to be travelling in.
4. Keep some cash concealed in your clothing (money belt etc) for emergencies.
5. Don't rush out and buy the cheapest travel insurance you can find, particularly if you are planning to travel to remote and/or dangerous parts of the world. Just because a policy states that you are covered for medical expenses up to £8 million doesn't mean the insurers will automatically pay up. It's wise to check not only the small print, but the reputation of the insurers and the company they use to undertake medical repatriations in the event of you requiring an air ambulance. Having broken my spine in a fall in Siberia I have some experience of this!"

Bryan Alexander, photographer, Arctic Photo, www.arcticphoto.co.uk

Travel Checklist for British Citizens

1. Check the travel advice pages at the FCO for the country you are visiting. You can sign up for email alerts for the latest updates for that country.
2. Register with the FCO's LOCATE service so it can get in touch with you if something goes wrong
3. Check the FCO website for the number of the nearest British Embassy and consular office to where you will be. If you are not a

British Citizen, find out your own Embassy and Consulate. Store their phone numbers on paper and in your mobile.

4. Know the number of emergency services for the country to which you are going. For all EU countries, this is 112.

5. Get good travel insurance—make sure it covers you for any activities you are likely to undertake, such as extreme or water sports. Always talk to the insurer (or ask someone to do so for you) if you are ill or have an accident. Never attempt to arrange your own repatriation.

6. Make sure your camera equipment is fully insured.

7. If you are travelling within the Eurozone, get a free European Health Insurance Card (from the Post Office or online at *www.ehic. org.uk*) for free or reduced cost of emergency care. You will still have to pay something unless you have private insurance.

8. Check with your doctor as soon as possible to find out if you need any vaccinations before you travel.

9. Make sure you've got correct visas for the country you are visiting and that your passport is valid. Some countries insist your passport still has six months or a year to run. Check entry requirements before you go.

10. All first time British adult passport applicants must now attend an interview to verify their identity. It now takes up to six weeks to get a first passport. For more information see *www.direct.gov.uk*

11. Take photocopies of your passport and other important documents and keep these separate from the originals when you travel (preferably keep one copy on you at all times) plus store copies online using an email address you can access from anywhere via the web or secure online data storage site, like *www.dropbox.com*.

12. Fill in the emergency contact details in your passport. This will make it much easier for the FCO to contact someone if necessary.

13. Tell a friend or relative where you are going and for how long for-give them some idea of your itinerary if possible and an emergency contact number.

14. Take enough money for your trip and some back-up funds in a mix of cash and travellers cheque–make a note of the cheques' numbers

before you go. Consider buying a pre-paid card, onto which relatives can also load money if you are stuck.

15. If you intend to drive, ensure your licence is current and valid. Make sure you are aware of the driving laws in the country you are visiting.

Top ten tips while you are away:

1. Think about what you are doing at all times and trust your instincts—don't take risks that you wouldn't at home.

2. If you are taking pictures of people, even with a long lens, you will probably be spotted. Ask permission first and smile…

3. Find out about local customs and dress, behave accordingly and obey local laws —there may be serious penalties for breaking a law that might seem trivial at home.

4. Check whether it's safe to drink local tap water—if not, stick to bottled water even for brushing teeth, and avoid salads, non-peeling fruit and ice in drinks. Make sure hot food is hot, cold food is cold. Tepid rice and soup that has been sitting around cause some of the biggest problems.

5. Be careful when taking photographs, videos or even using binoculars. Such activities may be misunderstood, especially near military installations

6. Take a mobile. A cheaper local call option is to buy a local SIM card, though make sure your phone is unlocked so it will work. This does mean your mobile number will change for the duration. You can buy a super-basic handset with some credit on it. There are also global SIM cards which will work in most countries. The article on *www.moneysavingexpert.com* has good advice and recommendations.

    If you are intent on keeping your number, check with your service provider that your phone will work. Many require you let them know if you are going abroad. Check their rates for not only making calls but receiving them as well. Texting is always cheaper or sign up for international access numbers with a company like Jajah Direct, *www.jajah.com* or *www.planet-numbers.co.uk.*

The Bigger Picture

7. You should beware surfing the web or receiving downloads on mobiles while away—you could come back to a huge bill. Switch off the data roaming facility.

8. If taking a laptop, you should be able to use wireless hotspots at libraries, airports, station and internet cafes, free or for a small fee. McDonalds offers free internet access. Be very careful using open hotspots—criminals love them as they can use illegal software to access your computer from theirs.

9. If you need to call home, Skype, via the internet, is free although you have to agree a time to call and the receiver must also be on Skype. Not every internet café will have Skype. You can also sign up to Skype's internet to phone service.

10. If travelling to remote regions, try and go with someone else and/or get a good local driver/guide or invite a local photographer.

Your Camera or Your Life

It goes without saying that if someone does try to rob you, it is better to hand over your cameras than to risk your life. One photographer, after being robbed in South America, was stranded half way up a mountain with no cameras, money or phone. He now always keeps a few bank notes in a secret pocket in his belt and a second mobile in an inner pocket. Another photographer keeps an old wallet with a few notes and out-of-date credit cards to hand over if mugged. He also has two mobiles: a cheap basic pay-as-you-go with a local sim card and his main mobile, hidden in an inner pocket. He always keeps camera memory cards in an inner pocket—cameras are replaceable: his photos are not.

Safety of Your Equipment

As airlines become stricter on size and weight of cabin luggage, photographers wanting to take a lot of gear have a dilemma. Airlines vary in the allowances for cabin luggage they give you, and it varies again whether you are flying economy, business or first class. Few photographers will risk their valuable equipment to be checked in the hold of the plane. Very few insurance companies will pay up for lost or damaged photographic gear if it has been in the hold and baggage handlers are not known for their care with suitcases.

Do check the airline's website well ahead of travelling, as some allow only one bag and have a very small dimension and weight allowance for cabin hand luggage. You do not want to have to repack and put your cameras/ lenses in your suitcase at check in for hold baggage or even leave expensive stuff at the airport. Some airlines have a frame, into which your bag must fit to be allowed as cabin luggage. Others will check by eye but just 1cm over could be a problem if they measure the bag. Weight is another problem. Some airlines allow you only one small cabin bag, maximum weight 13lbs or 6kg in economy class.

One solution is to wear as much camera gear as you can. Invest in a jacket or fisherman's/photographer's vest with lots of deep pockets. Wrap your lenses/ camera in bubble wrap and carry them on you. You have to take the cameras or lenses out for security checks but you can then repack your camera bag once on board. Some airlines refuse to have tripods or monopods in the cabin, so pack these in your checked luggage and pray your suitcase arrives at the same place as you.

All photographers need to consider their fitness and the physical demands carrying gear imposes. Although camera equipment now weighs a great deal less than it once did, it can still be a burden after a while. You may also have to carry a laptop. A backpack distributes weight better and puts less strain on one shoulder. If the backpack also has a waist strap, so much the better. The straps should be padded and wide enough so they do not cut into you.

Small Gifts Open Doors

Handing out money on demand is not recommended and in some countries, both children and adults will demand payment for being photographed. While most photographers will not pay cash, small gifts, such as pens, post-cards of the UK, keyrings, badges, cards etc., may get you the shot. Some-times, showing your camera and then taking a shot and showing the results may be enough. But if it is not, no shot is worth getting into real trouble. If someone says or indicates 'no' to being photographed, walk away.

Appendix

Magazines worth looking at:

AV (For business managers needing audiovisual): www.haymarket.com

BFP Market newsletter (for members of the Bureau of Freelance Photographers): www.thebfp.com

Black and White Photography: www.thegncgroup.com

Digital photographer: www.imagine-publishing.co.uk

Digital SLR Photographer: www.dennis.co.uk

Digital SLR User: www.bright-publishing.com

www.F2Freelancephotography.com

Image Magazine: www.the-aop.com

Master Photographers' magazine: www.thempa.com

Photo Pro magazine: www.bright-publishing.com

Professional Photographer: www.professionalphotographer.co.uk

Source: www.source.ie

Portfolio Catalogue: www.portfoliocatalogue.com

HotShoe: www.hotshoeinternational.com

Next Level: www.nextleveluk.com

British Journal of Photography: www.bjp-online.com

Photo District News: www.pdnonline.com

Online photography magazines, many with a fine art photography bias:

www.seesawmagazine.com

www.1000wordsmag.com

www.purpose.fr

www.vewd.org

www.ahornmagazine.com

www.deepsleep.org.uk

www.lensculture.com

www.fstopmagazine.com

www.blueeyesmagazine.com

www.blur-magazine.com

www.fractionmag.com

www.zonezero.com

www.filemagazine.com

www.dazeddigital.com

www.flakphoto.com

http://lab.colorsmagazine.com

www.ojodepez.org Version in English and Spanish.

Documentary/photojournalism/press:

www.enterworldpressphoto.org

www.lunaticmag.com

www.socialdocumentary.net

www.boston.com/bigpicture

www.burnmagazine.org

www.coloursmag.com

www.the37thframe.org

www.viiphoto.com

www.photoeye.com/magazine

www.foto8.com

Other useful websites:

www.pfmagazine.com

www.deviantart.com

www.snappershack.co.uk

www.ephotozine.com

www.photosites.co.uk

www.photographydirectory.com

www.freelanceuk.com

www.photographers.co.uk

www.fashionphotographyblog.com

www.talkphotography.co.uk

www.photopromagazine.com

www.photonet.com

www.professionalphotographer.co.uk

www.theprofessionalphotographer.org.uk

www.ukbusinessforum.co.uk

www.recontres-arles.com

www.rapideye.uk.com

www.photofusion.org

Industry directories

For lists of suppliers, support services and other industry contacts and to get yourself listed as a photographer:

Creative Handbook: www.chb.com

The Marketing and Creative Handbook: www.mch.co.uk.

Creative Match: www.creativematch.com

Trade shows

www.focus-on-imaging.co.uk

www.photokina-cologne.com

Photovision: www.forwardevents.co.uk

Index

Lightning Source UK Ltd.
Milton Keynes UK
UKHW02f1829081117
312394UK00012B/1343/P